Poetry Ireland Review 123

Eagarthóir / Editor
EAVAN BOLAND

Poetry Ireland Ltd/Éigse Éireann Teo gratefully acknowledges the assistance of
The Arts Council/An Chomhairle Ealaíon and The Arts Council of Northern Ireland.

LOTTERY FUNDED

Poetry Ireland invites individuals and commercial organizations to become
Friends of Poetry Ireland. For more details, please contact:

Poetry Ireland Friends Scheme, Poetry Ireland, 11 Parnell Square East,
Dublin 1, Ireland

or telephone +353 1 6789815; e-mail info@poetryireland.ie

FRIENDS:
Joan and Joe McBreen, Desmond Windle, Neville Keery,
Noel and Anne Monahan, Ruth Webster, Maurice Earls,
Mary Shine Thompson, Seán Coyle, Henry and Deirdre Comerford,
Thomas Dillon Redshaw, Rachel Joynt, Helen Flanagan

Poetry Ireland Review is published three times a year by Poetry Ireland Ltd. The Editor
enjoys complete autonomy in the choice of material published. The contents of this
publication should not be taken to reflect either the views or the policy of the publishers.

ISBN: 978-1-902121-67-3
ISSN: 0332-2998

ASSISTANT EDITOR: **Paul Lenehan**, with the assistance of **Matlyn Drucker** and
Natalie Lewendon

IRISH-LANGUAGE EDITOR: **Caitlín Nic Íomhair**

DESIGN: **Alistair Keady** (**www.hexhibit.com**)

COVER CREDIT: from *A Girl 2* by **Kanami Hana** (**www.sofinearteditions.com**)

Contents   POETRY IRELAND REVIEW 123

Editorial

COLLABORATE

Some years ago I was teaching poetry to a large group. At the front of my class was a profoundly deaf student who attended with two women who signed the class for her. This student was always present, always engaged. I made sure to be in her clear line of sight so her signers could bring the class to her as quickly as possible.

Quite often students brought in their own favourite poems. One day she asked if she could bring in a sign language poem. The following week she did. The poem she chose was printed on a page which was copied and handed out. Then she presented that same poem through sign language – a beautiful choreography of voice – through her signers – and hand gestures. It was intensely moving.

The students were galvanized – drawn in as I was by the courage and composure through which limitation had become an unlimited aesthetic. But more than that. They were also struck to be watching a collaboration between two languages: the auditory reading of the poem and the visual language which was signed – the two translating each other to further texture and depth, a collaboration as old as poetry, reaching back into its associations with music and magic.

Collaboration is not a word that is associated with poetry as readily as it is with music, drama, or the visual arts. Certainly when I was young it was strongly suggested that the best, if not the only collaborative project, was the encounter between poet and page. Which of course remains central. But it seems to me that something is lost if past and present collectives and collaborations are not brought back to be part of the conversation.

For example, there was the 1930 Surrealist experiment known as *Ralentir Travaux* (Slow Down Men Working, in English) – a series of poems written over five days by André Breton, Paul Éluard, and René Char. The three men met in Avignon, and worked in the Rich Tavern. They drove together around the Vaucluse, talking, arguing, composing. And the title of the project came from a road signal they glimpsed on the way to Caumont-sur-Durance – a reminder of just how improvisational collaboration can be.

In pre-modern Japan there was the *Renga*, with its chain linking and multiple authors, from whose first stanza, the *hokku*, today's *haiku* emerged. Or in the contemporary moment, American poets like Matthew Rohrer and Joshua Beckman, whose 2002 volume *Nice Hat* was a mutual writing project. Their comments remain relevant: 'We've always been interested in collaboration and the idea that being an artist or a writer in a community becomes a form of collaboration – not just working in dialogue with people, but actually writing with them. We also thought of our audiences as collaborators.'

In Ireland, editing *Poetry Ireland Review*, I'm often struck by separate energies that don't quite intersect, but yet are clearly present and seem to promise good things to one another if they only could engage. On the one hand there is the page: the values of the hermetic poem are at the centre of all poetry. Page poetry will always rightly shelter the private poet who seeks a reach and distance in their work that keeps it at angles to public statement, or the expectations of an audience.

On the other hand, the vivid forays into the public poem represented both in the US and Ireland – and many other places – by collectives such as Spoken Word have energized and given power to new definitions of the poem and the poet. New relations with the audience have emerged from this, which are in fact contemporary revisions of the old relations, where the poet spoke with and for that audience.

Yet despite these excellent energies, there remains almost everywhere – in the US, Ireland, the UK – some tension, some suspicion, between the poets of the page and those of performance or the public poem. They are not divided by acrimony but by custom and tradition: deeply layered choices and commitments that not only change the poem but also the identity of the poet.

In the US, even on a campus, I can hear these suspicions expressed on both sides. The performance poet, whose connections with an audience are deep and sustaining, can feel that the contemporary moment is theirs in a unique way, that they should be allowed to refresh outdated curricula, revise subject matter, and challenge the academy. The page poet can feel – and sometimes say openly – that the public poet is exempt from the challenges and nuances of private work, of words and forms whose life on the page has a more testing and more timeless relation with the reader.

Both make important points. But it seems to me at times that their mutual suspicion might stand in the way of something valuable: a meeting point where these historic formations in poetry might actually find one another and share their energies. That certainly would be a worthwhile and exciting collaboration.

– **Eavan Boland**

Nan Cohen

A LIKING FOR CLOCKS

After spending so much time looking
into their faces,
how could I not love them?

If they were not there,
I looked around anxiously
to find them,

not changing, but doing
the same thing over and over

in different rooms
on different days.

I looked to them to tell me where I was,
how close to the next moment,

and if sometimes I was impatient with them,
that is little to how they delighted me
with the promise of each new hour.

They were steadfast whether someone was
dying or being born,
arriving early or late.

When I began to slip through time
they looked at me with what I thought was sorrow,
and then I thought I saw them look away,
like friends who can't bear to watch your mistakes.

Eamon McGuinness

A GIFT

There are battering, low moments
but at times I think it's a gift,
as I cycle past the hospice,
how he didn't end up there,
that it didn't turn into home-
help, live-in carers, daily visits.

I see myself turning into him.
Those dead-air smells of novel reading
on the toilet before bed, mid-week
weekend newspaper catch-ups, setting
the table at night for tomorrow's
breakfast and shushin' on the headlines.

I missed summer that year,
while autumn came with dust
and trailing winds which woke
me, with empty fire-
place noises and someone
downstairs stealing his things.

Afric McGlinchey

IN AN INSTANT OF REFRACTION AND SHADOW

A plane floats overhead,
lethargically as feathers.
Egyptian cotton billows.
A train somewhere whistles.
You aren't happy, he tells me,
until you consider yourself
happy.

The afternoon light is falling
in a diagonal the length of the floor.
An arrowed line
of black gunpowder.
I follow it, feel him
brace for it, my familiar cry ...
and then I'm migrating, I'm gone
and there's only grief here.

Mara Bergman

THE NIGHT WE WERE DYLAN THOMAS
 – *for Suzanne Cleary*

In ways we were a most unlikely group: Mark engaged
and David with his thick moustache and beard, you
a sophomore and me in my first year, our friendship
sown in a farming town, upstate New York,
in stark-lit rooms and the Rathskeller where
one Friday afternoon we drank pitcher after pitcher
of beer and one by one composed a line and passed it on
until it grew … incomprehensible. More unlikely
was that summer's night on the Upper East Side
we converged to eat spaghetti. Was it David's
or Mark's idea to hop a cab to the Village,
the city singing, the driver speeding
to the heaving bar on Hudson? Was it you or Mark or David
who propped an elbow on the counter, looked up
to strike that pose? Then the rest of us in turn, unlikely
as it was even to be there, not that anyone seemed to notice
or care as we paused and waited, one by one, for someone
to click a camera and make us famous.

Joseph Horgan

ART HISTORY OF EMIGRATION

It is strange
that we hang
in dark suits
and v-neck *geansaí*,
our ties and black shoes,
rows of us
along the wall
and in the foreground
our uneven townland
of space-black drinks,
our collars
and hardened hands
in framed perspective
always reaching out
across the copper dented tables,
the impression and colour
of wordless listening,
to an indifferent sea.

Maria Johnston

AGED EAGLES

Michael Longley, *Angel Hill* (Jonathan Cape, 2017), £10.
John Montague, *Second Childhood* (The Gallery Press, 2017), €11.95.

'If I'd known I was going to live so long, I'd have taken better care of myself.' The words of the great stride pianist Eubie Blake were quoted with
delight by Michael Longley at a public reading on the theme of 'Ageing
and Memory' in Dublin last year. I can't bear the thought of a world
without Michael Longley in it, yet his poetry keeps hurtling towards that
fact more and more urgently as it stretches in an unflinching way beyond
comfort or certainty. 'I wouldn't mind dying now, I think, / Shutting
at last my bird-watching eyes', he admits in 'Bird-Watching', one of the
most moving poems in his new collection, as it lurches between sleep
and wakefulness. Death looms large, moving contrapuntally against the
surge of life that is augmented, amplified, by attentive searching. 'We've
been out in the fields all our lives, heads / Down, looking on the ground
for larks' nests', the opening poem, 'The Magnifying Glass', concludes,
with a downward tug that is felt across the whole collection even as the
lark ascends. That this opening letter-poem is penned to fellow poet-
ornithologist Fleur Adcock should be noted. I've written elsewhere on
the importance of women poets to Longley, among them, Barbara Guest
(whose poem 'Otranto' gives life to Longley's 'Cowslip'), and in *Angel Hill*
he converses with a range of female life-forces, including Kathleen Jamie,
Dorothy Molloy, Gwen John, Edna O'Brien ('the other Edna'), and his
daughter, the painter Sarah Longley. Even granddaughters, new to the
world, play a starring role: in 'Nativity', little Maisie shines as the Virgin
Mary armed with an 'antique spongeware bowl' that is 'still unbroken /
After birth-pangs and stage-fright and / Large enough to hold the whole
world'. That bowl seems an ample metaphor for her grandfather's life's
work.

 'Too late for orchids now', the poem 'Kindling' laments, or is it? A
page later the same regretful motif has wafted into 'In The Mugello' ('We
are too late, my love, / For the lizard orchids), which itself looks back to
'Lizard Orchid' from 2014's *The Stairwell* – the poet 'All ears in the Mugello'.
Such a chain of echoes in succession foregrounds the poet's flair for
invention and reinvention. If we read a poem like 'In the Mugello' as a
rewrite of Robert Lowell's 'Skunk Hour' (relocated to Tuscany) and hear,
in the repetition of that 'too late', Louis MacNeice's elegy 'The Casualty',
we find ourselves lifted off in a way that is profoundly revivifying. Surprise
is never far off and two of the book's most riveting poems are 'found'.

'Telling Yellow' takes the words of the painter Winifred Nicholson and magicks them over the line-breaks until,

> ... all my yellows broke
> Into luminosity.
> Orange and gold
> And primrose each
> Singing its note.

Nicholson's work was recently exhibited alongside that of her painter-husband Ben (they painted side by side), and it is marvellous to think of the poet taking these words from that context and allowing them sing in a new way across the fret-board of poetic form. As this collection signals, the figure who remains central to Longley's own artistic life is his wife, the critic Edna Longley. Marking their golden wedding anniversary, a selection of poems pay tribute to her as steerer and sounding board:

> You have pointed out, like a snail's shell
> Or a curlew feather or mermaid's purse,
> The right word, silences and syllables
> Audible at the water's windy edge.
> — 'FIFTY YEARS'

'We borrow their eighteen-carat love' – the anniversary gift 'The Ring' makes the temporary suffice as the poet holds up to the light a ring 'worn / By a Tommy fighting in the trenches'. War haunts the death-suffused *Angel Hill*, and a poem about Apollinaire's love letters (Longley's to Edna were 'randier') recalls something Longley once said about himself with Apollinaire's ability to 'write love poetry in the shadow of death' in mind: 'I don't want to be thinking of myself as an older poet, and I don't want to be too conscious of my own processes.' Yet throughout, Longley nods to his own processes in a piercing way. 'Your subject matter is sheep in a field', he writes to Sarah Longley, but could be addressing himself. The sonnet 'Memory' commemorates where 'I wrote my first poem that was any good, / "Epithalamion", rhyme-words dancing / Down the page ahead of the argument'. This form of self-criticism reminds us of Longley's own prowess as a critic, not only of literature, but of the visual arts.

Indeed, his description of Odysseus in 'The Brooch' as 'talking about himself again / Telling the truth and telling lies', may be a sideways glance at his own strategies as a self-conscious artist of similarly 'intricate craftsmanship'. In 'The Necklace' we overhear him remarking to his wife: 'Long ago I compared us to rope-makers / Twisting straw into a golden cable.' All of the expected themes are here in *Angel Hill* but with a twist as the line between the critic and the poet Longley is deftly blurred and selves multiply then disappear. Amid poems lost and found, there is the poet himself, deliberately flitting in and out of view, as if in a hide tracking himself over time. The elegy 'The Ornithologist' – 'Counting and re-counting / The generations, listening / For their messages on the wind' – reads as a covert self-elegy, another veiled self-portrait in a book that meditates on the art of portraiture. And if the 'he' of 'The Ornithologist' overlaps with the 'I' of the poet-ornithologist, then that sense of impending loss is the reader's own:

> I don't want him to walk away.
> I'll follow him to the Saltees.
> We'll ring all the cormorants there.

'How can I count the colours?' Longley asked in 'White Farmhouse', an elegy for the artist Colin Middleton from *A Hundred Doors* (2011), and as the poet orchestrates the poem that moves in time the acts of counting, re-counting, accounting for and making count, are key. 'Where is he now?', he asks in 'Storm', his elegy for Seamus Heaney; 'Together / We are counting tree-rings.' Although the final poem in *Angel Hill* leaves us with the birds' flight-form as an 'image of poetry', it is the closing frame of 'Age' that stamps itself with desolate perfection on the mind's eye: 'I walk ever more slowly to gate and stile. / Poetry is shrinking almost to its bones.'

Among the writers who converged in Heaney's house on Belfast's Ashley Avenue (its demolition painstakingly rendered in Longley's 'Storm') between 1968 and 1972, was John Montague, who recalled 'the crackle of gunfire in the distance' at that time, and Montague, who died last year, will always be read as one of the eminent poets of the person in, and up against the ravages of, history. 'Wind-wounded, lop-sided now' (to quote again from Longley's magnificent 'Storm'), Irish poetry is bereft of Montague now too and *Second Childhood*, published posthumously, seems a fittingly idiosyncratic coda for a fosterling poet who thrived on the periphery. As Eiléan Ní Chuilleanáin wrote of him back in 1989: 'Strangeness, restlessness, a more pressing urge to be elsewhere, put him outside the general chorus'. I'm still figuring out what Montague intended when he assembled this book. Although billed as 'a collection of new poems', many of the stand-out poems are anything but new. For instance, these unforgettable lines from the poem 'Riddles' –

> Who has a mother
> but is motherless?
>
> Who has a father
> but is fatherless?

– appeared in the title essay of his 1989 collection *The Figure in the Cave*. As he wrote in that essay, the answer to the riddle is 'myself of course; losing a family and a country in one sweep must not have been easy'. It's as though he is, from beyond the grave, sending us back to certain talismanic texts to ensure that we do not forget the reach of his art and his place/s in the world: 'My amphibian position between North and South, my natural complicity in three cultures, American, Irish and French.' In this way, those riddling lines send us beyond the specifics of family out into the world of poetry – to John Berryman, Ezra Pound – to Montague's four local masters, Hugh MacDiarmid, Robert Graves, David Jones, and Austin Clarke, to Gerard Manley Hopkins, and of course to Yeats as 'our great father figure'. As a final signing-off, *Second Childhood* showcases his interactions with many of these figures as well as with the dolmens of his childhood. As far back as 1988 he spoke to Dennis O'Driscoll of a long poem called 'The Great Bell' which he was working on. *Second Childhood* closes with 'The Great Bell' – his record of years conversing with David Jones – finished now and having previously been published by Enitharmon Press in 2015.

'The Leap' is perhaps the most skilfully executed poem in *Second Childhood*, and it too has lived a life before, appearing many decades back in Montague's 1988 collection *Mount Eagle*. Brought back into the light in this new context – it closes Part One of the collection – 'The Leap' now reads, as it perhaps didn't before, as a poem about death, and readers will certainly read it with the poet's own death in mind:

> no longer young –
> I take your hand
> to face a different
> more frightening task:
>
> [...]
>
> using a lesson learnt
> long ago in Lynch's meadow,
> circling the task
> to vault the flow
>
> and taking off again
> into the uncertain dark,
> hoping to land safely
> on a far warm bank.

In this acrobatic feat of analepsis, as throughout the rest of *Second Childhood*, we feel ourselves constantly on the cusp, jolted over the line-breaks and the artfully-placed sectional and stanzaic pauses. Born in 1929 in Brooklyn, the young Montague was weaned on the cinema and the effects of this early immersion are felt through his manipulative way with poetic form. The impetus to constantly return, to revisit, rework, is all over this last goodbye. In 'Return' (the title of which points back to another poem with the same title from 1962's *A Chosen Light* as well as to *The Rough Field*'s mantra 'in all my circling a failure to return'), a reference to Shelley's unfinished masterpiece *The Triumph of Life* shows how much of this is a calculated *au revoir*. Revisions are vital to the work as life's work. After all, to revise is to be alive and subject to change. 'Sad friend, you cannot change', Elizabeth Bishop reminded the dead Robert Lowell. 'And in that instant did I become a poet?' the poem 'Return' asks. So many of the poems here are about poetry itself and the process of becoming a poet: the sonnet 'New Milk' could be an *ars poetica* with the all-seeing poet 'shy, but bold / enough to entice'.

'In retrospect you create your own childhood,' Heaney once remarked, and *Second Childhood* reads as an attempt to, not recover, but re-place, re-frame. That the book cover features Kate MacDonagh's 'The Mask', places the focus firmly on the stylized persona of the poet, and, by extension, to Yeats's poem 'The Mask'. That lasting image from 'Riddles' of 'a small boy / standing in a field', endures in the way that Berryman's alter-ego Henry in 'Dream Song 384' still stands above his 'father's grave with rage', and asks, 'When will indifference come?' 'My work is riddled with human pain,' Montague told Dennis O' Driscoll in 1988. *Second Childhood* expands on that definition to embody the energies of artistic (re)vision. 'In retrospect, I can now acknowledge the influence of *The Rough Field* on other books of mine', Ciaran Carson has observed, noting its 'obsessive circling around themes of exile and identity, its concern with language and music'. Montague's influence as a poet is irrefutable; his obsessions were inescapable. 'The music I prefer, it would appear, is that of infinite variation', he wrote in 1971. To read Longley and Montague is to follow the lead of two masters of song who combine music, memory and infinite mischief; both, in the manner of Longley's dipper, 'wild and melodious', in their own incomparable way. To leave the final word with Montague: 'turn the lights down, and that music up ...'

Harry Clifton

THÉRÈSE AND THE JUG

> *Marriage is the monastery of our time*
> –Leonard Cohen

She liked the jug, because it was cracked.
If it had a flaw
It was perfect. Under God's law
It was made whole by what it lacked –

Or so you tell me, matter of fact,
As you water a whiskey
Last thing at night, or sweeten Darjeeling tea
With the milk and honey of tact.

How many decades now
Since we entered the enclosed order
Of ourselves, to raid and replenish the larder
Of imperishables? The marriage vow

Grown ordinary, seems to keep house
And break bread with us, through and through,
At communal vespers for two
Like a hidden spirit. Patient Thérèse,

Our patron saint of the infinitely small,
Examines the wedding plunder, stainless steel,
Anything bedsheets might reveal
The morning after ... Total recall,

If it ever came, would be shattering as a mirror
We stand before daily,
Man and wife, success and failure –
Childless love, imperfect as a marriage

Or that fissured jug, its flaw that integrates
A world around it, so you say,
A world left behind, for the Little Way
Of ovulins and fetherlites.

Simon West

Walking above a bluestone bridge I tilt
against the rails. I watch its trickling stream
trying to conjure sentenced men who built
this crossing and set my stage – mid-nineteenth
century men, hardened by exile till
they shed the burden home set on their dreams.
My ancestors, my house whose memory
is stunted like the broken bole of a tree.

On my mother's side, out from County Clare
came Ellen Smith – illiterate, eyes: green –
a widowed dairymaid who stole a cow.
Complexion: pale, one child in charge, R.C.
She wed in Hobart Aaron Hibbard: collier.
Head: small, complexion: swarthy, C. of E.
Whether their lives blazed or were cold as slate
the only records now are those of the state.

I try to kindle names with facts, or chart
a distant origin: from York, Carlisle,
Northumberland and Kent. Places I'd learnt
in Shakespeare's worlds, swapped for this sceptred isle
where outcasts nursed the wounds an Empire's blunt
blade dug in a demi-paradise
of postcard pastures with their docile game,
a wound that festered past the change of name.

Death wiped a shipwrecked generation's slate.
Their children seemed to spring from wind-tossed seed
and grew staked to the mores of English state.
My grandmother denied her convict breed,
kept corgies, never uttered words like *Mate*.
She found no cause to doubt the proper creeds
or think Fitzgerald's might be built on sand.
One never dwelt on tribes who'd lost their land.

The stream below says make your ancestors.
Choose that wild goose John Boyle O'Reilly, shipped
to a land of Oyster-and-Ale. Take poets who sought
to shape examined lives in song. Their gifts
are prayer and tribute, just as fleeing Troy
Aeneas shouldered father, son and Lares.
And before your own transport to fog-thick seas
cling to the past and sing its legacies.

Maresa Sheehan

OUR LAST DAY

You collected me off the train in your Daihatsu Fourtrak
made for cattle and dirt with moss on the window rubbers

with mam not home, you asked, will we go to the chippers?,
plumpness only got you snogs from fat boys, but I was starved

we ordered two burgers and chips in the 'Friendly Fryer'
she shouted "I can do you another burger for nothing if you'd like?",

over the frenzied chips in the fat, the mincemeat
gulping and gasping on the hot plate

the snack box meal picture desperate to be noticed by day,
you'd know by her she hated waste, "it's our last day,

the health inspectors are closing us down" and she gave us
our brown bags, the fat making them shiny on our laps

as we laughed and blew and ate and waved the heat
and said how would anyone say such a thing?

we can still laugh at that,
my mother mostly answers the phone now.

Niamh Boyce

HANS ARDENTLY COLLECTS PATIENTS' ART WORK

Heidelberg Asylum, 1890

i once had a sister

Agnes, Laundry Number
583, embroiders phrases
'from her disturbed mind'

onto the bodice, sleeves
and cuffs of a jacket
cut from asylum gowns.

i once had white stockings

Confined to the ground floor
she threads each eye, pushes
needle after needle

stitching *ich ich ich* ... out
side and in, till linen
whispers *meine meine*
meine to skin.

Alan Titley

MAOLRA SEOIGHE
  – a crochadh san éagóir de dheasca ár Mhám Trasna 1882

Ghluais tú tríd an oíche shíoraí
Áit ar thrasnaigh na mathúin an sliabh
Lena ngeaitirí beaga den dlí a chuir lasadh
Leis an móin fhliuch a raibh taithí agatsa uirthi.
Is tú a fuair na clocha beaga crua ag feitheamh
Sna tithe móra nach bhfaca tú riamh roimhe
Go dtí lá beag sin na cearnóige féasóigí
Nuair a bhí peiribhiúic ar an bhfaiche
I bhfad níos fairsinge ná guth fann na fírinne.

Is ea. Níor thuig tú go raibh ór sna bailte agus
Sa bhéarla sin nár airigh tú riamh cheana,
Go raibh daoine gan puth anama ina suí
Ar phrócaí meala a ghreamaigh dá n-intinn.
Intinn álainn mós simplí a shealbhaigh do chorp,
Seantuiscintí a choinnigh comharsana ó scóig a chéile:
'Ná goid, ná santaigh cuid do chomharsana,
Ná maraítear duine ar bith, ná crochtar fear
Chomh neamhurcóideach leis an leanbh sa bhroinn.'

Proinsias Ó Drisceoil

UNSETTLING THE WORLD

Biddy Jenkinson, *Sceilg* (Coiscéim, 2017), €10.
Aifric Mac Aodha, with translations by David Wheatley, *Foreign News*
(The Gallery Press, 2017), €11.95.

Biddy Jenkinson is renowned for her refusal to have her work translated
from Irish into English. Her refusal to be translated has not simply been
an issue of language affirmation; it has done much to determine the character of her work. As a result of being published solely in Irish, her work
can share a cultural understanding with her readers, as well as sharing a
range of allusion – native saints, legendary heroes, literary texts, songs in
Irish, traditional phraseology and sayings, for instance – that might well
prove perplexing to a transnational audience. Her refusal to be translated
may well be a form of liberation.

In her poem 'Eiléana in Pláka', the Greek resort immediately sets her
mind racing over songs in Irish with Greek allusions:

> Iníon rí Gréige
> mar chéile leapa leat,
> A Dhónaill óig ...

'Scál' in the collection's title, *Sceilg na Scál*, means both 'supernatural being'
and simply, 'person', and in a series of nineteen poems, the first section
of the book, the poet imagines life as lived by monks who are now just
a ghostly presence on the renowned hermitage, Skellig Michael, off the
Kerry coast. Her imaginative engagement with the rock and with the life
once lived there is witty and self-deprecating without being irreverent,
and while her engagement with the history of the place is a profound
one, personal concerns cannot be avoided:

> Soipríonn clocha na gclochán
> isteach le chéile
> chun díon a choinneáil ar an saol
> tamaillín eile.
> — 'SOSCÉALA'

Short lyric poetry as written in Irish during the period of monasticism,
as well as traditional forms such as the triad, impact on Jenkinson's own
approach to composition, as in a terse poem where she removes a limpet
from a rock to become herself the one grazing. Poetry becomes her
perimeter:

In Éirinn
bíonn imlíne ar an dán.
Anseo, an dán an t-imlíne.

Ar eagla mo chaillte
bogaim bairneach den leac
agus suím ina áit
ag iníor.
                    –'LIMISTÉIR'

Her poetry has a developed, recognisable style that frequently favours
the short unrhymed line. A chatty informality which often involves a
direct speech quotation or an address to the reader is also a hallmark, as
in 'Hósana sna Bánta:'

A Bhríd,
ón uair nach ndéanfainn
deimhin de dhia,
ní den loighic é gairdeachas a dhéanamh leatsa ...

The title of this poem invoked the phrase from the Mass, 'Hósana sna
hArda', one familiar to many speakers of Irish and is one of several allusions – 'staid na ngrást', 'oirniú, 'Peaca an tSinsir', 'Úll na hAithne' –
which presume a ready acquaintance with Christian and Catholic heritage,
as indeed did poetry and art in Europe generally, until recent times.
    Jenkinson's poems range across many locations and concerns. 'Uab-
har' summarises the life-affirming character of the collection with opening
lines that declare that she spends her life humbling herself before all that
there is. This, for her, is poetry's essential purpose:

Caithim mo shaol ag umhlú dá bhfuil ann.
Nó sin is filíocht ann, dar liom.
Agus shíleas nach raibh aon ní beo,
nó neamhbheo,
nach n-umhlóinn dó.

Sceilg na Scál is an extensive collection, and the first published by the
poet since *Oíche Bhealtaine* in 2005, although she did publish a long poem,
Táinrith, in 2013. The poet herself has painted the attractive artwork
reproduced on the book's cover. Appropriately, it shows cormorants on a
tide-lashed rock with a cross inscribed, no doubt off Skellig Michael.
    If the phrase 'translated by David Wheatley' on the cover of Aifric
Mac Aodha's new collection gives the impression of a plodding retainer
faithfully replicating in English original Irish poems, then it is wholly

misleading. Wheatley's task in conveying into English Irish originals that are as multifarious as they are personal was a formidable one, and he has a particular difficulty to contend with in the debt owed by the original Irish poems to poetry in English, and to the shape-changing jokiness of Paul Muldoon in particular. He meets the challenge with versions that wrestle with the Irish originals while simultaneously expressing Wheatley's own aesthetic; yet the verve and grief of the original poems persists in the translations, and Wheatley is frequently mischievous in his interpretations, most cheekily when the sole line in English in the original, *'No thanks, I've read the Bible'*, is 'translated' as: *'If that makes me Adam, then you must be ...'*

Mac Aodha's favoured form is the sustained series of linked poems with an overarching theme. Her major themes include loss and transience, growth and metamorphosis, but while a biographical basis to these doubtlessly exists it is never made explicit, being transmuted instead into an energy and emotion which defines these poems. The influence of Muldoon is made explicit in the poem titles, 'An Dara Plaic, nó Ath-Quoof 1'/'The Second Mouthful (Quoof: Slight Return 1)', and 'An Tríú Plaic, nó Ath-Quoof 2'/ 'The Third Mouthful: (Quoof: Slight Return 2)'. These are poems that have their being within language and many of them play effectively on sound similarities: 'riadaire'/'radaire' for instance, with their unconnected meanings ('elder', 'ranter'), or éislinn'/'éist linn' ('unsafe place, 'listen to us'), both from 'Gó'/'Chicane':

> Éislinn gan chosaint
> an éist linn dúchais

> The unguarded tongue needs
> someone to come to its aid.

In 'Cailín Bréagach na mBráithre'/'The Brothers' Little White-lie Girl,' the word 'dícheall' carries the simultaneous meanings 'best endeavour' and 'neglect', the latter now largely a literary use. In the ambiguous line 'gurb ionann dícheall agus dícheall', footnote numbers are impishly attached to both instances of the word 'dícheall,' but no footnotes appear! Lines such as 'gur fhadaigh tost an béaldath,' ('Sop Préacháin'/'A Crow's Wisp') where 'fhadaigh' carries the meanings 'lengthened' and 'ignited', are untranslatable, but Wheatley comes close with 'how silence improves lipstick'.

The poems embrace the entire vocabulary of Irish but do so without being abstruse or obscure. In form, the poems draw eclectically from the Gaelic literary tradition, and while unequivocally modernist they simultaneously owe a great deal to medieval and early modern metre and poetic form: the succinct *burdún* and *dánfhocal* forms in particular gives the poems concision and lyrical grace, as in these lines, also from 'Gó':

> Tabhair meilte
> ar na blianta a lean,
> ar an gcuthach ceilte
> a d'éirigh ina bhean.

> Grind down to nothing
> the years still to come,
> the hidden fury that's grown
> into a woman.

As with much of modernist literature, the poems draw promiscuously on mythology and folklore, and the collection is heavily indebted to Greek and Old Irish mythology. 'Gabháil Syrinx,' one of the shorter poems in the collection, derives its lyrical power from the story of Syrinx's transformation into a musical reed as she eludes Pan's advances:

> Anáil mhná, ní scaoileann
> ach eadarghlór ar tinneall:
> i láthair na gabhála,
> ceiliúrann sí is critheann.

> A woman won't breathe
> unless ready, between words:
> at the site of ambush
> she sways, transformed.

The Old Irish tale of adventure, 'Echtrae Conlae', provides the title and framework for a meditation on voyage and passage but, in line with the modernist character of the collection, the poem is equally informed by Joyce's story, 'Eveline,' which shares its themes of choice and risk.

The books title, *Foreign News*, like its contents, is capable of multiple interpretations, and the choice of a bullfight painting (*Seville* by James Hanley) to illustrate the cover is equally enigmatic. Perhaps image and title combine to suggest that poetry in Irish comes from outside as an unsettling challenge to the settled world of poetry in English.

John D Kelly

THE RED GLOVE

So this is how
our local row concludes –
with weapons
not yet finished still of use?
I always thought
that a newly-wrought sword
could not be held
when it first left
the forge
and that blunt lie-cast words
(my love)
could never fell me
or that their faint echo within
the white-bellowed roar
of your fire – heard by me
now – could ever cut so deep.

Yet as my tempered blade
now cools
in snow
from tip to hilt –
beside my ebbing rage –
I no longer have a need
to hold it
or use it
I no longer have the strength
or desire to lift it
as my own blood congeals
on your fine asbestos-lined glove.

Eva Bourke

SMALL RAILWAY STATIONS

As far as they were concerned, Ionic porticos
had not been invented, pillars or rosette
windows, marble, mosaic – they left all this circus
to the important stations in the cities
with their tracks to far-flung places
where passengers sat in the waiting rooms
their eyes on the hands of the huge brass clock –

no, the small stations were low, built of blackened brick,
a box of pansies their sole embellishment
on the sill where the cat slept.
Inside, the windows were the undisputed domain
of the common house fly. News from nebulous distances
ticked on the telegraphs; the tapes grew and curled unread
till they reached the floor. Poppies flourished between the tracks
and if you put your ear to a mast
you could hear an insect swarm at its core.
The stationmaster's red cap glowed in the sun
like a warning signal. Never did the express to the capital
stop here, but carriages of local trains
followed the slow curve down the valley
behind an engine that puffed and whistled in protest.

It's years since the small stations were erased from the maps
and closed down. They are pizzerias now, sports bars,
youth clubs; nothing happens here, no more departures,
tears, welcoming embraces. But once I found myself
in a café in one of those forgotten stations
and on the platform saw the place name: Langendreer –
this was the station where my mother had left
for her studies in a remote city.

She must have stood here between the wars waiting for the train,
in her burgundy coat and black velvet hat,
a serious young girl with a small cardboard valise beside her.
She was spirited from here to other stations, more momentous
than this one, she was blown farther
and farther away into the disasters and joys
of her time, its terrors and solemn moments,
with nothing but her light luggage.

Catherine Phil MacCarthy

LEGACIES OF EMPIRE
 – in memory of Michael Davitt

1.

Can you create a sketch within the space
outlined in red pencil of Ireland with
'landlordism' become a kind of blight?
On second thoughts, a winged vulture,
that throws a shadow across the land.
The sketch should be made in India ink,
to print well in photographic presses.[1]

2.

It was said by old people who mind
the year he was born, that the starving
were found on the sides of roads,
in the fields, once or twice on the street.
Mothers with infants in their arms,
children, hand-in-hand with father,
sometimes a toy, a puppy in their grip,
all their belongings heaped on carts,
walked mile after mile barefoot
against the clock of an empty gut.

1. Letter from Michael Davitt to Sarah Purser, dated 16 September 1890, held in The Manuscript Room, National Library of Ireland.

Richard W Halperin

THE BEACH, MALAHIDE

The sea green and grey that day.
She told me two or three frightening things
which had happened to her over the years,
and one sad thing. I do not know
if the sea helped or if I helped
but something got transferred. Later,
over tea, she said, "Now you know."

The middle of any story is always missing.

Little boy blue becomes old man blue.
Fin d'histoire.

Matt Kirkham

KURT RESPONDS TO ADELE'S CALL TO REMOVE A SPIDER FROM THE BATHTUB

On which foot does consistency begin?
His self-doubling self-doubting shadow

chitters about nothing more than itself,
and can grip each successor-of-zero of his feet

as well I can write the bathtub's equation.
Reading the spider, the metamathematician

says he's a metaphor for nostalgia,
a child's game. Which tiles on the floor

can you step on without disaster?
Think slippery nebulae, the maps

of all the worlds you see in those puddles.
A metaphor for nostalgia for metaphor.

You'd like to see the spider's feet as points
of a compass rose, but they spin

like a universe without time. And as soon
as you turn he slips down the wall.

Susan Lindsay

WHEN THEY'VE GROWN ANOTHER ME

on a petri
what a dish
that will be

they took a picture
of my passport
in the Building Society,
my mobile phone number
to allow them send
me code numbers to ensure
extra security to add
to the other questions
all of which could be
answered by anyone
who cares to do a little research.
It makes your
on-line presence more secure.

My identity on-line
is now a product
my profile
a saleable commodity
I get no payment for.

My Revenue number, once private,
alongside the mug shot
taken to ensure
de-person-al-isa-tion
on the card, my pass
to free transport
that has me turn to writing verse
restrain myself
from cutting it to pieces
it should come with a government
warning: this could damage
your mental and physical wellbeing.

When will 3D printed bones and organs
supplant the you

you once were?
When the only thing left
to identify me distinctly
is my DNA
and they take a sample
of that and grow me
on a petri dish
for stem cell research
or to have a copy
in case they lose me
will there be anything left to lose?
To whom will I
belong?

Who or what
kind of a dish
will that one be?

Jaki McCarrick

MAN'S WORLD

Pete Mullineaux, *How to Bake a Planet* (Salmon Poetry, 2016), €12.
Noel Duffy, *Summer Rain* (Ward Wood Publishing, 2016), £9.99.
Patrick Moran, *Bearings* (Salmon Poetry, 2015), €12.

Pete Mullineaux's fourth collection, *How to Bake a Planet*, which also includes six songs, has about it a blithe, minstrel quality; but make no mistake, the poems here are taut and possess a razor-sharp wit as they take on, either directly or tangentially, subjects as diverse as residential nursing homes ('The Light'), animal welfare and climate change ('Chicken Song', 'Careful what you wish for Orangutan'), equality issues ('Zola Budd awaits Roger Bannister on Mars'), and contemporary politics ('Jeremy Corbyn – Weapon of Mass Destruction'). What ties the various themes together is the merciless relish with which Mullineaux explores them, which of course only adds to the humour in his work.

The collection begins inoffensively enough (a false sense of security perhaps) with a series of poems about relationships. In 'Small Hungers', a pair of lovers' 'ravenous toes' embrace each other, while 'Love Bites' explores a first love. Then it's on to 'Fair Way' about a top golfer who 'chokes' in an important tournament due, the speaker believes, to a childhood trauma. It says a lot about Mullineaux's philosophical outlook that he finds such relatable material in the sportsman's failure. By the aforementioned 'The Light', about life in a nursing home, Mullineaux's political sensibilities are in full-swing and we become, like the poem's speaker, enraged by this institution (a generic place, familiar to anyone who's ever visited a nursing home) that closes its curtains by 6 p.m. so as to be 'Safer by far', and where Sky News is 'on an infinite loop of toxic negativity'. With this poem, Mullineaux brings his audience straight into the beleaguered present, and from here to the end of the collection the poems interrogate the many political and social problems of our age. Social isolation in particular is explored, as in 'Rest Assured' and also in 'Fatal Distraction', in which train passengers are 'buried in a laptop, cross-word, romantic / novel or magazine', oblivious to 'wildlife or the human kind', while in the song 'The New Launderette', the speaker declares, 'In a world full of people you've got no friends'.

A favourite of mine is the long poem, 'Zola Budd awaits Roger Bannister on Mars', originally written as a response to a prompt from the *Guardian* Poetry Workshop (which was to place two historical figures in an unlikely setting). Via an imagined meeting on Mars between the eponymous athletes, Mullineaux's poem explores the legacy of Budd, who still holds a British record for the mile race, as compared with that of Bannister, who, in 1954, ran the first sub-four-minute mile. Budd, famous for running barefoot, became entangled at the 1984 Olympics with her American rival, Mary Decker, in the 3,000 metres final, resulting in Decker's fall. While Budd's sporting achievements have been largely forgotten in the haze of controversy about that race, Bannister's reputation continues to soar, his achievement 'a moment inscribed like a needle spike in a cracked record'. It's a cutting line (whether intended or not), one that is especially relevant today, in that it acknowledges how female athletes often receive far less attention and acclaim than their male counterparts. A probing, beautifully written poem, instructive in its fascinating subject matter and rhythmically taut, here Bannister is the 'long-striding golden boy, languid in / his authenticity', while Budd wonders:

> ... Would we have been suited, one of my names a French
humanist, one of yours a handrail?

A spiky tribute to Jeremy Corbyn is also a gem here: in 'Jeremy Corbyn – Weapon of Mass Destruction', the poet constructs a wry takedown of those in the Labour Party who plotted to destroy this 'dark knight', for whom 'so-called ordinary citizens have voted' in Corbyn's constituency of Islington 'thirty-two times'! Here the speaker declares:

> He'll blow
us all into next week, lighting the fuse as we speak;
this is not baloney – take it from the trusted lips of
Gordon, Neil and yes, Tony. The fiend ...

In his poems, Mullineaux goes from a tidy free verse to the villanelle, as in 'Inflation Theory' and, in 'Broccoli – a meditation on paranoia', to quatrains. He's at home in all forms; though I think the stricter form suits him and forces a compression upon his considerable rage. His interest seems to be more often in subject matter than in language, though his skill here is significant. In 'High and Low Roads', a striking meditation on the roads out of Galway into Clare, the speaker observes that 'A heron awaits us, still as death'; in 'First Fruit', about biting into a tomato, he describes 'seeds scattering / like electrons whirling at the / speed of light.'

The six songs at the close of the collection are just as incisive, though more loquacious, as if written for the protest march or soapbox. They include a gloves-off assail on the 'Shell and government hand in hand' arrangement on the Rossport pipeline in 'Disconnect Song', and in 'Dinosaur's Lament' we are face to face with the poet's despair at the stupidity of mankind, fast engineering its own extinction.

Both poems and songs are peopled with easily recognisable characters: young lovers, famous sports people, travellers in a queue at airport immigration, the residents (or inmates perhaps) of a nursing home, customers in a launderette, the elite of the British Labour Party – and so this collection has a familiarity despite its political commentary. While Mullineaux has rightly been compared (in a previous review of his work) to John Cooper Clarke, due no doubt to his socio-political subject matter and frequent use of rap rhythms (and there's the punk connection, too: Mullineaux's song 'Disposable Tissues', written in the mid 1980s, was composed in support of the women's camp at Greenham Common and later recorded by punk outfit, Pete Zero & the Options), his work also re-calls John Clare. Like Clare, who wrote about the destruction of his part of Northamptonshire in the wake of the acts of enclosure, Mullineaux seems compelled to record perceived injustices, as in his pieces about the Rossport pipeline, Greenham Common, and the sidelining of Zola Budd.

Noel Duffy's third collection, *Summer Rain*, comprises three distinct sections. The first, 'Games of Chance & Reason', a Vienna-based dramatic piece, primarily about the relationship of physicist Ludwig Boltzmann – who arrived at his theory of statistical mechanics in the early twentieth century, anticipating Einstein's paper on Brownian Motion by a year or so – with his harshest detractor, Ernst Mach. The second section, 'Into the Recesses', is a series of poems exploring the cycles of water, and the third, 'Summer Rain', is a sequence of Dublin-set monologues. The first two sections have recurring scientific references in common (Noel Duffy is a physicist) – while the third doesn't explore the subject of science at all. However, the three sections do cohere, mainly due to the atmospheric, introspective tone to the writing in all three.

The Boltzmann drama, 'Games of Chance & Reason', is a fascinating story, one that is worth revisiting (perhaps even in novel or play or screenplay form). Though Duffy tells it succinctly, such is the power of the images, characterisations, and short scenes here, that this poetic drama alone might have filled his collection (if not that novel or screenplay). The denouement is powerful and incredibly moving. Readers not versed in the history of scientific concepts and their originators will learn a lot from this opening section, while the statistical mechanics theory and other hypotheses are 'explained' here in a clear manner, as when Boltzmann demonstrates entropy to his students by shuffling a deck of cards, initially 'in perfect sequence / suit by suit':

> 'This simple trick demonstrates my concept of entropy:
> how an orderly state will always return to a more
> disordered one, my shuffling of the cards the action
> of time on a system. It is the natural law of things.'

In 'Into the Recesses', Duffy brings his scientific thinking to bear on the natural world, and in these poems the distinctions between the elements are emphasised ('the kingdom of water, / the kingdom of air'), providing the work with an intense, distilled quality, reminiscent of Alice Oswald. The titles here are also a successful means to bolster the middle section into becoming the strong centre of this three-part collection: 'That Which Lives Within', 'That Which Lies Beneath', 'Shapes That Fit Together', *et cetera*. My favourite of these water-themed poems is 'The Leap', about the salmon and 'their passage upriver'. The salmon's life, the speaker declares, is 'a life-sapping assault of current and granite'.

The collection's last sequence is comprised of ten present-day monologues from Dublin-based characters. For the most part these are powerful and affecting, particularly, 'Frank', the story of a promising son lost to drugs; and 'Caroline' (about an artist), which contains the arresting lines: 'I will paint / the smell of rain instead and start / with earthen brown and red.' It's from this exuberant piece that the title of the collection (and sequence) is presumably drawn:

> I so love the rain
> in summer, the way the smell
> of earth creeps up from the garden
> and catches in the nose, a dark,
> rich charcoal.

The themes explored in Duffy's collection can be identified early on, in 'Games of Chance & Reason', when Boltzmann's student Lise declares 'An ordered state is becoming / a more disordered one' – *i.e.*, the notion of order and disorder is examined, how life is constantly in a state of flux at a microscopic and macroscopic level. Duffy's language is tense and taut, which, combined with his honed (scientific) way of observing, often creates a haunting quality in the poems, as in these first lines from the imagistic 'Cloud Reflected on Water':

> The bowl of the sky
> is cupped in the lake's basin,
> the upper world projected
> down into the recesses

While Mullineaux loudly shakes the gates of 'the system', the patriarchy, Duffy explores its structures at a molecular, more hermetic level.

Also a third collection, *Bearings* by Patrick Moran is an encounter with life in contemporary small-town semi-rural Ireland. Moran's territory is that of Patrick Kavanagh's – had the latter remained in Monaghan – and, of course, been alive to note its changes:

These hi-tech farms sprouted from hoed drills,
straining horses, pits, ricks and roosts.
                              – 'HERE'

The poems here have, overall, an unapologetically boozy quality to them;
they explore a 'man's world' of bars, snooker and pool rooms, bed-sits,
afternoons watching sport (in pubs, naturally). This subject of the slightly-
at-odds (with everything) Irish male is a rich vein for Moran, and in this
collection he mines it particularly well.

In 'Yield', the speaker is driving home from work when a falling leaf
jolts memories of boyhood; likewise in the poem 'Polar', in which a
memory stirs in response to the image of a polar bear on a TV programme.
In 'Kindling', a night's drinking, after the 'rambling soliloquies / on
thistly pastures, / unbedded women', inspires the speaker to go home
and write, while in 'Graveside' a local farmer's funeral becomes a terse
portrayal of the man's life. In 'Faith Healer', a now dead 'character' of the
town is brought to life via an enquiry about her house. These are fond,
non-judgemental examinations of the lives of real people in that much
opined place, 'forgotten Ireland' – lives made valid and rich in Moran's
moving collection.

A wonderful poem here is 'Ferment', in which the poet turns his sub-
stantial empathy towards the abuse victims of recent church scandals; it's
a heartfelt three-stanza elegy in which the speaker imagines his subject as
a child in an orphanage or institution of some kind, listening out for the
'sandal-squeak at midnight'. That's a really harrowing line, but one which
conjures the horror of the abuse perfectly, without being explicit.

Like Kavanagh, Moran sees the extraordinary in the everyday, thus
this collection is a fine document of contemporary Irish life away from
the metropolises and hubs, 'on the edge / of calculated farms, / newfangled
bungalows' ('Nocturnal'), where the pulse of the area is the 'neon- / lit
takeaway'. His is a delightful 'booze-charged voice' – but like Noel Duffy,
Moran's use of language is beautifully precise. There's 'a fraying drift of
midges' from 'Journeys', and 'mute, ubiquitous / blightings' from 'Har-
vesting', and the pithy 'treachery of ice', from 'Black Ice'.

All three collections here display a confidence of voice. There would
also seem to be in each, to a varying degree, a questioning of the role of
men and masculinity in a world where formerly stable patriarchal structures
are no longer (quite rightly) being allowed to rest easy.

Stav Poleg

LISTEN, YOU HAVE TO READ IN A FOREIGN LANGUAGE

Read it like poetry – don't expect
to understand everything –
fill in the gaps with your own
half sentences. Don't read translation
theories. Just don't
treat a language as if it's a precious
vase that could break
any second. It is a precious vase. It breaks
while we're talking – that's why we fall for it and
with it, and – listen – you have to
think for yourself but in more
than one language, and yes – life is
an exercise in freethinking, and yes –
a different language could make you
furious at first – and isn't it
strange? But so many things
can happen: the moon, a Pegasus wing
at your door, a telephone ring
(and you know who
I'm thinking), the sky making
no sense. So many things
may never. But listen – don't listen
to me. Listen to yourself. You wouldn't
believe it.

Noel Monahan

TWO WOMEN AT A WINDOW

A response to Bartolomé Esteban Murillo's painting

The two of them are looking out at something
Or someone. The younger lady leans forward,
Hand supporting her chin, shoulders bare,
Blush of rose to mark her bosom, bronze braid
Catching the folds on her dress. The older lady
Holds the shutter ajar, stretches her head shawl
To cover her nose and mouth. We can only guess
What's happening
                              On the street below.
The funny bits of the day: young men throwing
Kisses up at them, Don Andrés walking his dog,
The barber-surgeon crossing the street for another drink.
On the other hand, they could be laughing at me
For staring at them. The older lady thinking I'm hilarious.
The younger just amused.

Stephen Spratt

SUBJECTIVITY

indigo   blue

      dream   schemed

         masterclass   chance

           perversity   diverse

             opportunity costs   forests

               migration   starvation

           fake news   news

     enemy of the people   people

     people   enemy of the people

           news   fake news

               emancipation   decapitation

           justice   self-interest

         sense   dissonance

      revenge   avenge

    trivial   all

end

AB Jackson

THE MERMAYD

The Voyage of St Brendan

The helmsman screamed. A creature swam in view,
obscured by wave blink, sun jinks, true-untrue.
A wonder for sure: woman / fish, hirsute,
she circled their boat repeatedly and mute.

Brendan yelled, "Brothers, do not tremble!
Tom, stop gnawing that wooden spoon handle.
The Cog survives on pickled Providence,
curried leather. Quit this flapping nonsense."

In swift response, the mermayd – as she was –
flicked her tail, dove down, consumed by froth.
The crew fell silent, all famished and well-fed
as she gurgled her throat-song from the sea bed.

Cathi Weldon

IN THE KEY OF ALZHEIMER'S
– for Deirdre and James J McAuley

You are gone
from my language sphere
to a newfangled space.

For decades we anchored
our childhood
in words, lodged

our loves, our moments
all debates, into
a common hoard.
The echoes, odours, pixels

that you draw on now, drift
out of sync so that
our histories incline
like ghosts to invisibility.

A memory recurs, slips
fritters asunder. It finds
no grip in your being
as you stray

to a station beyond
concious orbit – where only
a white cat roves. You

who have lost my name

stay me with tenderness
and from your core
produce a dulcet sigh.

John F Deane

OLD BONES

I, John, I was on the island called Inishmurray ...

There was a sense of Genesis to it, Alpha moment,
morning sun over the waters off Mullaghmore, boat-engine idling
while we sat on fishing-boxes
and relished the yapping of waves against the hull.

Ben Bulben in the distance, slopes of sun and shadow,
sheltering Ireland's poet under her wings.
The castle, Classiebawn, loomed
as a dark landmark above the cliff, and we knew

these waters brimmed, not long ago, with broken thwarts
and exploded faith. For this is Ireland, holding her wars,
her poets, her ruins and her rains, and the holy islands
where we, the curious, come to pray.

★

Outside the harbour wall we pitched in unexpected swell,
Atlantic Ocean spray
blessing us with salt. Our touching on the island was
uneasy, without dock or quay, only the black rocks

slippery with weed and sea-wet. Herring-gulls barked
like guard-dogs and a kestrel,
fast as a prayer, flew by. I scaled a rock-trail through thistles
where the testy ghosts

wished to be left in peace. To this abandonment, friars came
centuries after the Christ, to forge
salvation, built rock altars, beehive cells, stone churches,
piled up their cursing-stones to keep

★

women and fiends at bay ...
What is it, then, of sea and sky and island,
of isolation and self-denial, that has left its caul
in my flesh and soul that I come

to scavenge here for understanding?
The black-backs watch, sharp-eyed and silent, shuffling
on the dry-stone walls, like monks restless in choir.
Within the ramparts of the enclosure

I sit, lost and at home. Out on the headland an old man plays,
off-tune, a slow lament:
'*an raibh tú ag an gcarraig*' and the sea responds:
a sigh and a withdrawal.

June Wentland

'THEIR WHITENESS BEARS NO RELATION TO LAUNDRY ...'

lard, onions, pastry,
cotton vests for a second baby.

Wind-picked rabbit skulls
and tic-infested ewes, have refused

to ingratiate themselves sufficiently
to be referenced. O for a knocked up

white with an improper hue
stolen from a blood-suckled

moon, tucked like a bump
up a jumper. White as a compound

too bulky for navvies to heave
from the slurp of the loam. Fractious

calcium, where skin chances on bone.
The pitch and resist of his cheek –

sticky as a fallen damson.

Note: the title of this poem is a line from 'Magi', by Sylvia Plath.

Louis Mulcahy

POTADÓIREACHT NA CAOLÓIGE

Over our door is a name
meaningless to most who pass.

On our arrival forty years ago
men who shouted dogs
to round up hillside sheep
could say who held each field
one hundred years before,
could tell their stories,
sing their songs,
relate their joys, tragedies
and occasional good fortune,
name their food, clothes, shoes or none,
their drownings.

They told who married in, who married out,
who stayed and hungered,
who, surviving steerage,
reached England or America,
to prosper or get lost in the attempt.
They could trace the name and story
of every field for miles,
how it was created, drained and tilled.
They knew the poets and fiddlers,
knew who built *naomhóga*,
best man to tell the weather,
the one to twist a *súgán* rope,
those who had the cures,
good masons for dry walls.

An *Caol-Fhód* –
narrow acre or narrow sod?
memories conflict –
one of four adjoining fields
known for soil and tuber,
generations having hauled and spread
baskets full of storm-ground sand
with rotted straw and rich cow dung
from the settlement
at *Cloichear* near its strand.
Traditions change,
An *Caol-Fhód*
not yet quite gone.

Harry Clifton

A SONG FOR EUROPE

Michael O'Loughlin, *Poems 1980-2015* (New Island Books, 2017), €15.

Michael O'Loughlin, like half of Ireland, was born and brought up in the kind of Irish space that has yet to find itself properly represented in anthologies and taught – or even acknowledged – in the colleges. It is not the rural space, colonised by Yeats, Kavanagh, and Heaney. Nor is it the inner city space of James Joyce or Sean O'Casey. It might better be described as a kind of migrant space between the two, of huge housing estates on the outskirts of urban centres, where generations of the economically dispossessed in the middle of the last century, uprooted from the one and ill-adjusted to the other, provisionally settled for the sake of work and family.

It was not, however – and this is important in the poems of Michael O'Loughlin – a specifically Irish migration. It had, in fact, been happening all over Europe since the late nineteenth century – a movement away from the land to the great and terrible cities, from the individual to the mass, from character to uniformity (those thousands of identical houses), from place to placelessness, and most importantly perhaps, from instinct to consciousness, the morally lonely individual cut adrift, or who cuts himself adrift, from inherited reflex values, and inhabits an interim space that is and is not Europe.

It is a feature of Michael O'Loughlin's work, and a distinction from that of almost all of his contemporaries, that it interests itself hardly at all in North America. We are all too used to the career move, the sabbatical in the liberal college, the award of uncertain merit that ventriloquises itself back to the home audience on the dustjacket of the latest volume. The zone of proxy war, the court of arbitration, the funeral parlour of the archive, carefully embalmed for 'posterity'. O' Loughlin proceeds as if this world, with its powers and nostalgias, is largely non-existent, or irrelevant at any rate to his own preoccupations.

Three key moments in the lifework are the arrival in Irish bookshops of the Penguin series of Modern European Poets in Translation; his move from the Dublin suburb of Finglas to the city of Barcelona; and his meeting there with Dutch-Jewish singer and writer Judith Mok, their subsequent life together in Holland and travels throughout Europe (he now lives again in Dublin). What matters is not the chronology but the mix of themes – Europe, Jewishness as identity, and the implied critique of Ireland as nation and culture.

Like many of his poetic contemporaries in the Irish Republic (the north, which features little in his work, had its own preoccupations), the new translated poetry offered him models of what a poet might be in a universe expanded beyond Irish nationalism and retrospect – the high rhetoric of Yeats, the cultivation of failure and passivity in the circles around Patrick Kavanagh. Militant communism (Hikmet, Ritsos, Neruda) and dissident anti-communism (Mandelstam, Akhmatova), fractured syntax and surreal, fragmentary lyricism (Popa, Ungaretti), Spanish *duende* (Jiménez, Lorca) and the more sober but open-formed voices of Montale or Machado, seem to have offered him the possibility of self-reinvention as a European poet in a stale Irish context, and liberated him to address not only the rootlessness of suburban space but subjects previously untouched, like the Limerick Soviet of 1919 ...

> And soon the sleeping suburbs will wake
> To the ragged secret chorus
> Of alarm clocks going off
> And people will march in their thousands
> Down the stairs in the still black
> Winter morning
> And lights spring on in the window of every kitchen
> Lighting up all over, the humble constellations
> > – 'LIMERICK, 1919'

... or not yet touched upon brokenly, Europeanly, like his rejection of a simplistic and imposed Irish tradition:

> When I got too old to fear them
> they appealed to a baser emotion;
> I was cutting myself off
> from a part of the nation's heritage
>
> But I didn't want to know their nation's heritage
> it wasn't mine
> > – 'THE IRISH LESSON'

Barcelona, the city he lived in and still returns to, has a wider significance, like Spain itself, as a place of change and awakening, moral, sexual, political, for Irish poets and writers from Pearse Hutchinson to Colm Tóibín, in flight from the oppressiveness of Ireland, as well as an ideal south of the senses and the possibility of an independence – Catalan – that opens rather than closes society, as happened in Ireland, and welcomes the exile rather than sending him into exile in the first place:

We sat once more in the gloom to sing some songs
And he strummed a simple melancholy dance
Over and over again, on the strung shell of an armadillo,
And falling through the years,
I saw a winter's morning of fear and booming voices
My hands cold clutching the varnished wood
While I painfully glossed a Gaelic poem
About a ship sailing out of Valparaiso
And how its purple echo had sailed with me
To this strange harbour, this unmapped land,
To dance now to the Charrango!

            – 'VALPARAISO'

That said, the true psychic landscape of this selection of his work is grey, flat, low-key, north European, still haunted (the base now is Amsterdam) by the remnants of the last war and the shadow of mass deportation, racial slaughter. Which brings us to the third key element in his work – the theme of Jewishness – and a curious inversion of the usual narrative in which Jews attempt to assimilate, to become German, French, Italian, and are subtly or violently rejected and thrown back on their old identity as victims and wanderers. In O'Loughlin the narrative is of an Irishman assimilating himself to Jewishness rather than the other way around. There is a self-identification with the exile, the wanderer, and a huge investment in a collective memory which is not his own. So many of his poems invoke Jewish victimhood, Jewish history, Jewish ritual that one cannot help feeling the identity of the poet has transposed itself from a given Irishness to a borrowed Jewishness, where, paradoxically, he feels more at home.

By eight in the morning in our basement kitchen
the ashtray was already full, and the coffee cold in our cups
as we talked of Bukovina and Paul Celan's last poems,
Scholem and the *Origins of the Kabbalah*.

Outside, it was still Ireland.

            – 'IN THIS LIFE'

Since the Eighties and Nineties, and a steady appearance of collections, his recent publishing history as a poet has been more sporadic, though the quality of the work is undiminished, sometimes stronger. *In This Life* (2011) was perhaps too small and quiet to garner the kind of larger consideration his work now needs, but contained the classic 'Elegy for a Basset Hound', one of those tender, private poems that belie the sometime abrasiveness of his public, poetic persona ('Other dogs feared you, perhaps rightly') and go a great way – the self recognising its own shadow, as Jung says – on the road to wholeness:

> And yet I loved you for something else:
> How on a brown December night
> When the light had soaked into the wet ground
> I saw you through the dusk of Utrechtsestraat
> With trams and teatime traffic crashing between us
> Out of earshot, almost out of sight,
> You turned on the crowded pavement
> And, like the old God of the kabbalah
> Lost in the darkness and unknowing before Creation
> You raised your nose and sniffed the fouled air
> And I knew that you had found me.

A writer or poet, Cyril Connolly once said, should be aware, as far as possible, of his or her 'latent curve of development'. That curve in O'Loughlin, through the angers and distractions of the years, looks increasingly like the circle Kavanagh describes, returning upon itself, but knowingly. There is an elegy, late in the book, to a fellow Dublin poet of the Seventies, Conleth O'Connor, a martyr to the suburban lounge bars, the smoke and alcohol mirages, that terrifyingly illustrates the failure to grasp oneself in time and get away, and which bears out, all too prophetically, these lines from 'The City', the opening poem of this selection.

> But too late you realize
> That you shall never leave here!
> This, or next, or any other year.
> You shall pass your life, grow old
> In the same suburban lounge bars
> Draining the dregs of local beers
> Fingering a coin in your otherwise empty pockets.

There, but for the grace of God, could have gone O'Loughlin himself. Instead, we have this fine retrospective, and the sense of a destiny comprehended.

Matt Bryden

THE LOOKOUT

Cataplanas in silver dishes –
a terrace in the canopied shade,
the two of us, this place
a dream state of white cloth
and breeze, the sea a stony field away.

Ambiguity hanging in the salt air.
Like two diners possessing precisely
the same likelihood of being
a couple, or father and daughter;
out there in the open.

Or a *vinho verde* the waiter opens, pours
and steps back from, complicit,
then collects the piled shells. Says,
"I can see you are resting, let me know
when you'd like coffee."

Even the crabs in their pots
fear the worst. They are through
with waiting – tired of banding
their own claws at depth
after three sharp tugs on the rope.

Orla Martin

THE POETS

There they are, The Poets.
Great at funerals, are The Poets.
Crumpled in pews, compassion by the verse,
by the haiku.
They do write a good card, do The Poets,
so they do.

Handy at weddings, are The Poets.
Meaning to the missalette, will they lend.
Happiness outside their comfort zone,
can stretch to contentment for a couplet or two,
before descent into Merlot infused ramblings
on life, on death.

In relationships, can The Poets be found, or lost.
Angled over pints in Grogan's or at The Library bar.
Intense over coffee, are The Poets.
Eloquently worded, grammatically correct sex texts,
The Poets do send.
On occasion.

For there they are, The Poets,
Cycling along the South Circular Road, a car they do not own –
they cannot drive.
They are there, The Poets, in sickness as in health,
in Tesco as in Aldi, in publication or rejection,
in darkness, as in light.

Catullus

'IF YOU'RE LUCKY YOU'LL DINE WELL'

If you're lucky you'll dine well,
dear Fabullus, at my place
any day now – if you bring all
the necessary; the wine, the multi-course
gourmet meal, not forgetting
your gorgeous blonde girlfriend,
the salt of your wit & all your raucous laughter.
So if you bring everything we will indeed dine well
for poor Catullus' purse is empty.
But in return for accepting my poor hospitality
you'll receive something even better than elegant kisses
for I will give you a divine fragrance
which my beloved was granted
by the true servants of Venus herself &
when you smell it, I swear by the gods, Fabullus,
your nose will blow your mind.

– translated by **Blair Ewing**

John Sewell

BEING ALIVE

Convinced every minute of the thirty years following,
that what killed him will, as night swallows day, take me too,

this morning I reached the age my father reached the day he died
to find myself still here, still fit, in apparent good health,

no signs I can't – touch wood, touch all in sight – go on savouring
for some time yet a glass of shiraz with my evening meal –

tonight, a dish of rainbow trout, courgette and Jersey Royals,
or sip a nightcap to the newly demobbed moon on Haddon Hill,

or best of all – the sun tomorrow morning stealing in
through the open summerhouse door to sit over me

take my whole naked body in its mouth.

Tess Adams

I HATE MY STINKING THERAPIST

        Yer man is acting out, playing
up, abandoning me to my demons, he's changed
our sessions messed them up, messed me up, he says
he's dealing with an elderly relative's illness, he says
he needs to make some slight alterations, he says
it like I'm a broken light bulb he'll get around to fixing
one day and I say that's fine, I can handle the break.

        To prove it I acquire another tattoo, a slithery snake
but then he tells me we're good again, we're OK
his sick elderly relative has passed away.

        And you know I'm glad about that, and then
I'm guilty for being glad about that, and then I'm angry
for having to feel like that, and in our next session he spots
the mamba curlicue across my hand (like it's hard to miss)
and he says: *OK, Let Me Have It*. So I do. I tell him I'm mad
with my mum, see the bitch left me when I was young ...
Oh Yeah, I def let him have it. Right?

Patrick Holloway

BARRAGE

Here is your poem
Stuffed with grief,
Oven grilled and crackling.
Glazed, glossed and gleaming
With stupid tears. Here is your midnight
Maddened poem that shines
Moon shadows sharp against the emptiness.
A suffocating space, laden with unlactated
Life; spoiled. A broody, broken, beat-down
Battering of words that fall like cement or disappear
Like air, words to paint the thick auburn
of your hair, the marble of your eyes. Failing,
Flailing, far-off words that I tear from me
In one quick strip. Words like screeching
And skidding and crashing. Onomatopoeic atrocities
That mean nothing. Words that brought me to you
And took you from me. Your rubbery skin and a doctor's
Breath at the back of my neck. His words that crawled and hardened
Inside of me. Did you know your wife was expecting? And his breath
Is still on my neck; I scrub but it lingers, like words, like a poem
Unread.

Eleanor Rees

ST. JAMES'S AT DUSK

Today the light is as faded as the sound
of the street above the cemetery.
A crow caws on its flight above our heads,
over the weight of bodies leaning into the dusk
until all of us are sinking in the rush of the afternoon.
A couple seen at the bus-stop, fresh from the train,
walk past again holding hands – we are still to meet.
And somewhere in the mush
freshly wrought beginnings rustle in their sleep,
dust off the damp of their winter coats, shake
plumes of curly hair and flushed cheeks,
walk along the track back up towards the mausoleum,
sandstone glowing gold as the sun sets
over the Welsh mountains'
burning snowy tops, light spooling out and across
the rocks which spin the red heat
like the hands of a clock.

Eavan Boland

JOHN ASHBERY (1927–2017)

John Ashbery was born in Rochester, New York, in July 1927. His parents
were fruit farmers, living and working near the cold reaches of Lake
Ontario. For all the deep interest in other cultures that came later, his
childhood was rural, quiet, and difficult. His father was irascible: Ashbery
would later describe his relationship with him as 'living on the edge of a
live volcano'. There was a certain isolation, perhaps compounded by the
gay identity he'd grow into, and the death of his brother from leukaemia
at age ten. In a late poem called 'The History of My life', he made a gesture towards that memory with the lines: 'Once upon a time there were
two brothers. / Then there was only one: myself.'

Ashbery's death in September 2017, at the age of 90, removed from
American poetry one of its strongest and most innovative voices. When
he was younger, and in a different time, it seemed improbable that he
would be so influential and so valued. There was a consensus that he was
a challenging poet. So much so that in his early career it was frequently
said that he had an audience but no public. By the time of his death he had
both. Even readers, who thought of him as difficult, came to see in his
work a fascinating mix of break-out radical and open-hearted traditionalist.

And for some he was more than that: for the experimental poetic
community he was the one essential figure who had envisioned the future
of American poetry. The poet Susan Howe wrote: 'John Ashbery was the
last great American Modernist poet living and writing here among us. I
feel lost without him.'

Years ago I drove down to Gorey to interview John Ashbery for the *Irish
Times*. He was reading that evening at a small festival. He was a courteous,
approachable man, with a surprisingly merry sense of humour and another
surprising layer of shyness. But he could also be blunt and dismissive. He
made it plain that he had no patience at all for such contemporaries as
Lowell and Berryman, recognised masters of lyric narration and personal
revelation, and validated at that point by fashion and the academy.

In that context, he made some memorable criticisms of the contemporary
scene. American poetry, he told me – and these are his exact words –
'suffered from the Cordelia syndrome'. All the varnished answers, he said,
were the wrong ones. Only the unvarnished were valuable. These remarks
were made when Ashbery was in his fifties, and starting to be heard.
They reveal the anxiety and resistance he faced when he began.

That beginning was marked by the 1955 publication of his first book, *Some Trees*, chosen by WH Auden for the Yale Younger Poets series. In his preface, Auden placed Ashbery in 'an important school of modern poets [that] stubbornly continues to live by the old magical notions'. The book is terse, but the magic is visible. Against the background of a conservative decade, the work demonstrated a maverick energy. In signature poems such as 'The Instruction Manual', Ashbery showed he could unite slang with the cadences of lyric statement; the knock on the door with the finest sense of doom; the occasional flash of an open space with a finished tableau.

> How limited, but how complete withal, has been our experience of Guadalajara!
> We have seen young love, married love, and the love of an aged mother for her son.
> We have heard the music, tasted the drinks, and looked at coloured houses.
> What more is there to do, except stay?

But for all that, it was not his decade. At least not in poetry. He once remarked that when he began writing poems in the Fifties, American poetry was formal and constrained while American painting was adventurous and experimental. In those years, Ashbery at the end of the day went to the Cedar Tavern in Greenwich Village. Poets and painters collected there: 'The artists liked us and bought us drinks,' he noted.

In fact, the 1950s was a time of discord in American poetry – a dissonance that would eventually open the way for Ashbery. The household gods of modernism were beginning to fall; Eliot's writ no longer ran; the spacious kingdom of nineteenth-century romanticism and canon-making was beginning to fracture into smaller, dissident fiefdoms.

Richard Wilbur (who died, aged 96, a month after Ashbery), won a 1956 Pulitzer Prize for *Things of This World*. Almost immediately, Randall Jarrell commented that 'Most of his poetry consents too easily to its own unnecessary limitations.' In 1950, Adrienne Rich became a Yale Younger Poet, her work also chosen by Auden. In 1956, Allen Ginsberg published *Howl and Other Poems*, further stressing the categories. In 1959, Robert Lowell brought out *Life Studies*. The decade ended with a cacophony. No one sounded like anyone else. Even so, in terms of audience and critical acceptance, by 1960 the field belonged to the very poets – Lowell and Berryman – Ashbery thought of as advancing 'The Cordelia Syndrome'. Ashbery's coterie of poets and painters would eventually be known as 'The New York School', though they were more like-minded friends than ideologues. But they were still on a margin at this time. It was difficult to be an experimental poet in a lyric age, and difficult to be gay. Occasionally the two came together. In an interview with *Time* magazine, Ashbery remarked: 'There is a school of criticism that says that my poetry is so torturous and obscure because I've been trying to cover up the fact of my sexuality all these years, and I think that's an interesting possibility.'

His remark is more than likely ironic – Ashbery was often droll and self-deprecating about his own work – but it tends to be forgotten now that his claim on a readership was extraordinarily slow. In the same interview he provided a startling statistic. 'It was a very long time before my poetry was first published and then read and then discussed. Those stages took decades, and it wasn't until I was about 40 that I felt that I had an audience. My first book only sold 800 copies over a period of eight years.'

Ashbery won a Fulbright scholarship to Paris and remained there ten years (less he says, for the intellectual atmosphere than the way of life), supporting himself by working as art critic for the *New York Herald Tribune*. There he encountered the work of poets such as Henri Michaux, and the enticements of surrealism. These he largely resisted. He once said that he was 'bored by the automatic writing of orthodox surrealism'. Nonetheless, he appreciated the glamour and importance of the surrealist perspective. 'I once interviewed the French poet Henri Michaux,' he said in the *Irish Times* interview. 'I asked him about surrealism and he said he didn't consider himself a surrealist but for him surrealism had been *le grand permission*.'

He had to wait for his own grand permission. It came after he had returned to the US, with the 1975 publication of *Self Portrait in a Convex Mirror*. The book won the Pulitzer Prize, the National Book Award, and the National Book Critics Circle Award. The title poem was especially eye-catching, and would come to define at least part of his achievement. It was constructed around Parmigianino's self-portrait – a painting Ashbery described as 'miraculous' – which, according to Vasari, scandalised and impressed his renaissance patrons. It signalled a different level of depth and ambition in Ashbery's work.

'Self Portrait in a Convex Mirror' is a dark, expansive speculation about selfhood and transcendence. There is a reach about it that is certainly elsewhere in Ashbery, but happens here with a special intensity:

> The pity of it smarts,
> Makes hot tears spurt: that the soul is not a soul,
> Has no secret, is small, and it fits
> Its hollow perfectly: its room, our moment of attention.

The poem is tightly woven. Though it attracted a new audience, it doesn't actually reach out to the reader but inwards to an elusive, often lost self. There are the usual sections of image and statement, but they never become anecdotal. The looping syntax is eloquent, but restrained. The poem's authority comes not from its signature style, but from its harrowing loneliness. It remains one of his finest poems.

But there were other moods, other moments in his poetry. A certain amount of it was playful, post-modern, resistant to so-called 'meaning': witty, wayward, and occasionally exasperating in its charm. His 2008 poem 'They Knew What They Wanted' – which is a cento entirely made up of quotes from other published works – has marvellous aspects of all of these:

> They all kissed the bride.
> They all laughed.
> They came from beyond space.
> They came by night.
>
> They came to a city.
> They came to blow up America.
> They came to rob Las Vegas.
> They dare not love.
>
> They died with their boots on.
> They shoot horses, don't they?
> They go boom.
> They got me covered.
>
> They flew alone.
> They gave him a gun.
> They just had to get married.
> They live. They loved life.
>
> They live by night.
> They drive by night.
> They knew Mr Knight.
> They were expendable.
>
> They met in Argentina.
> They met in Bombay.
> They met in the dark.
> They might be giants.

They made me a fugitive.
They made me a criminal.
They only kill their masters.
They shall have music.

They were sisters.
They still call me Bruce.
They won't believe me.
They won't forget.

The achievement of John Ashbery has to be seen against a background. He was an American poet. He lived an American life. He ascended to a commanding position in his country's poetry against the odds. After Ashbery's death, Paul Muldoon wrote in the *New Yorker*: 'Ashbery himself was the first to be amazed at how a figure who so resolutely argued against convention, the quintessential outsider, came to occupy a central position in American poetry.' But Ashbery's presence and influence also reached past national boundaries and local categories to generate a conversation about the future as well as the present of poetry. And yet the question remains: Why? This hadn't happened with the work of Lowell or Berryman, or even Bishop. No other poet provoked quite the same level of discussion.

So, why Ashbery? A simple answer may have to do with patterns in poetry itself. Its history demonstrates that while the centre may initially dominate the margin, the margin in the end almost always defines the centre. This is true as much for Gwendolyn Brooks and Adrienne Rich as for TS Eliot and William Wordsworth. Eliot's comments in 'Tradition and the Individual Talent' remain convincing. 'What happens when a new work of art is created is something that happens simultaneously to all the works of art which preceded it. The existing monuments form an ideal order among themselves, which is modified by the introduction of the new (the really new) work of art among them.' In every sense, Ashbery was the new, the really new.

And that remains an incomplete answer. Far more has to do with Ashbery himself. In the *Irish Times* interview, he gave a halting but accurate account of his aesthetic: 'I feel that what I'm perhaps trying to do is to portray time and changing, which I'm very much aware of ... How do I feel now? How do things affect me at this particular moment?' What made Ashbery so compelling to both readers and critics was his ability to braid together familiar strands of American poetry in an unfamiliar way. Although he could be a difficult writer, poem by poem, the braiding was lucid and visible. On the one hand, in terms of style and image, he was on the un-sunny side of Wallace Stevens: in that region where the Emperor of

Ice Cream, the jar in Tennessee, the river of rivers, were all dark signs of elusive meanings. Ashbery may have resisted surrealism, but his work is relentlessly disruptive of logic and his images are often fired off with surprising disjunctions and dissociations.

On the other hand, there was something else, something defining and notable. Which is where the braiding occurs. Unlike Stevens, Ashbery had no interest in oracular language. Instead, he was a self-styled master of the vernacular, a magician of the common speech, a fidget spinner of clichés. 'I'm attracted to well-worn clichéd language that has been used for ages,' he once said, 'when people are trying to express something that is really important to them, and thus it ends up sounding banal, which for me is somehow holy.' Behind that statement, behind the poems that embodied it, are important ghosts. Eliot of course, with the intimacy and irony of certain passages. But there is Whitman also. Ashbery referred to him as an ancestor whose 'barbaric yawp didn't impress me at first, but whose silken language did as I began to live with it'.

And so, a contradiction emerges, one almost unique in recent poetry. In his love for French poetry, his surreal affinities, Ashbery could appear a member in good standing with the post-modern mandarin group, a stylistic coterie that cared little for audience and resolutely disdained the search for so-called 'meaning'. But in his vernacular style, his superb championship of the common speech, the beautiful music of the familiar phrase that wanders radiantly through his lines, Ashbery emerged as almost the opposite: as one of the great democrats of twentieth-century poetry. The haunting and humane music of his best poems confirms that.

In the end, Ashbery also has to be seen against the background of an art that was going through its own ordeals. Modernism. Post-modernism. Revision of the poem. Even more revision of the poet's identity. Through it all, Ashbery was a steady presence, a laureate of the divided and compromised self, which at times seemed to be all the age had to offer. He accepted those divisions, those compromises. He was comfortable with them. They let him speak about the ambiguity of the self. He spoke in the words of his moment, without complaint, when he said in the *Irish Times* interview: 'I don't know what myself is. Myself is this person that I would very much like to know, and keep trying to get to know in my poetry but I always feel the truth of what Rimbaud said, for once and for all: *"Je est un autre"* / *"I is another"*.'

I can't believe I'm seeing this by **James Kirwan**
  Acrylic and spray paint on canvas, 31h x 23w cm
  www.sofinearteditions.com

The Falling of the Leaves by **Kanami Hana**
Woodblock, 25h x 25w cm
www.sofinearteditions.com

A girl 2 by **Kanami Hana**
Woodblock, 40h x 40w cm
www.sofinearteditions.com

Decomposition IV (After Rembrandt) by **Seán Molloy**
Oil and beeswax on wood, 16 cm in diameter
www.sofinearteditions.com

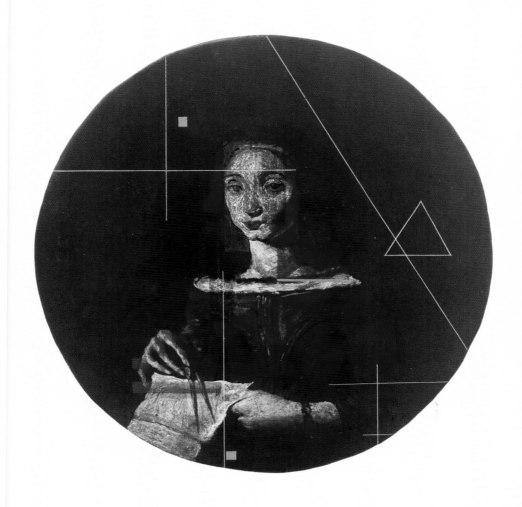

Decomposition XIII (After Pietro Paolini) by **Seán Molloy**
Oil, ink, and sgraffito, 16 cm in diameter
www.sofinearteditions.com

At least fail while daring greatly by **Clare Henderson**
Etching, 12.5h x 16.5w cm
www.sofinearteditions.com

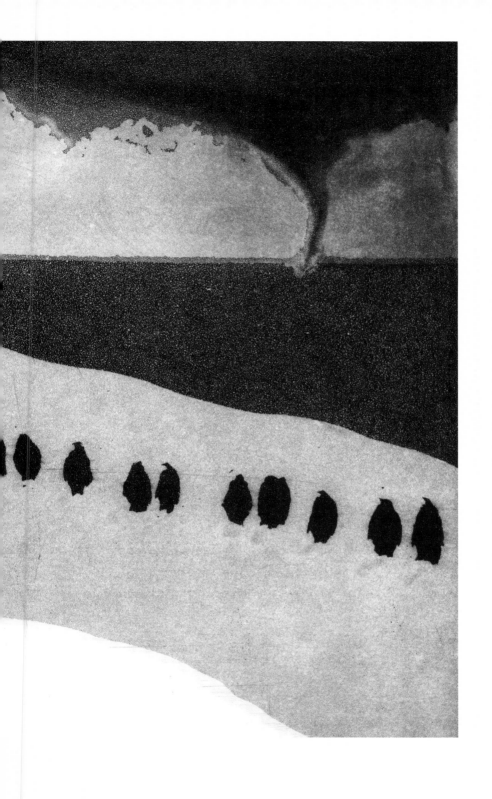

Enjoy the Flight by **Yoko Akino**
Photo intaglio, 20h x 19w cm
www.sofinearteditions.com

All the images in this issue are from artists who have exhibited
this year at SO Fine Art Editions, 10 Anne St South, Dublin 2
www.sofinearteditions.com
E-mail: info@sofinearteditions.com

Craig Dobson

WHAT'S THE USE OF MYTH?

Where there should be a man
sown in seal's skin, crowned
with bone from a sea king's cave,
his features inked with nymph spell,
his fist round a silver cup of storm and thunder,
his feet on tricks to charm an otter to the grave,
his eyes bound with dew, his mouth stuffed
with mermaid song, his ears full of bird call
at the blooded edge of dawn, as men haul him
to the torn cliff and the patience of the waves ...

where these should be, there's me,
turning the litter of a tideline over:
a length of nylon rope, plastic bottles,
one broken toy, a lone shoe's laceless eyes
bright among weed gobs and sea-worn bits,
the shards of crab and mussel shell,
the stinking ruin of a fish, this sea's dull
recession where indifferent gulls wade
silent, beyond by my halting progress
through the thin, grey fade of evening.

Francis O'Hare

I DID WONDER
– for Diarmuid Cromie

Remember us that August morning
nearly thirty years ago,
the sun already high and burning
in the blue air, clouds moving slowly through the summer sky
like cattle on some western prairie?

On the road, to Belfast, thumbing
lifts from traffic, like our heroes,
Kerouac and Dylan, bumming,
Dharma-style, a pair of hobos,
bound for glory like Woody Guthrie
and hungry for the future, Newry

fading in the dusty distance
like some old sepia photograph
of a mid-west town, a lonely train's
whistle like a dead man's laugh
our farewell message of goodbye,
fixin', as we were, to die

or die trying to make New York
or San Francisco; well, Belfast,
before the ancient highway broke
our youthful spirits or our last
cigarette got smoked, the empty
pack our will and testimony.

Well, anyway, the sky was blue
and walking wasn't suffering;
a friend to share the road with, you,
the high school football-god, blithe morning
bright with birdsong. bee-hum, me
the dreaming poet; suddenly

a car slows down on the A1's edge
and a door opens. We jump right in,
not taking time to think or hedge
our meagre bets, or even question
who's offering this charity.
This was God's hand. Destiny.

And that's the way it was. Our lift
turned out to be a man of God,
a minister and his wife, both soft-
ly spoken, sincere, kind-hearted,
asking about university,
recommending their church's chaplaincy

and generally passing the time until
the skyline of Belfast appeared
like Gotham City; huge, dark, still,
in the front windscreen. Were we scared?
Excited? Well, we smelt the sea,
heard the gulls, sensed that we

were entering a New Orleans
and maybe were a little nervous
about the prospect, the midday sun's
rising shadow ominous
as we drove into the glaring city
full of tension, hope, anxiety

leaping up like buildings, tall
and full of windows ... then, remember,
the wife's lost words that said it all,
down by the docks, "I did wonder ..."
as we thanked them for their help, the high
cranes like statues, things of beauty.

Sighle Meehan

POST EXIT

When you were born I moved into the slow lane
tucked my Jag behind a Škoda
buckled every harness,
sometimes in my rear-view mirror I glimpsed
a girl speeding round forbidden bends
towards equal pay and status in the boardroom,
sometimes someone glinted on the fast lane
someone racing towards the tip of Everest
sure she'd get there fast.

As we chugged the growing years
on scooters, pedal bikes, taxi fares to broken curfews
I learned the strength of violets
in the lower ditches, primrose clumps
near dusty tarmac.
One day, somewhere, a Ferrari revved
I saw your eyes change gear
saw you take the outside, charge
the open road.

I stalled, pulled in, swiped
at moisture on my windscreen,
hunkered in the shelter of low stonewalls
as lightning cracked the tree tops
opened up the skies
          jet acceleration, freeways overhead.

Martin Malone

THE DUSTY ROAD

Frank Ormsby, *The Darkness of Snow* (Bloodaxe Books, 2017), £9.95.
Katie Donovan, *Off Duty* (Bloodaxe Books, 2016), £9.95.

Fifth and sixth collections from well-established poets probably ought to
be satisfying affairs which see them build assuredly upon what has gone
before. And, pleasingly, that is what we have here. These are two fine
books, worthy of our attention, from poets in winning command of their
craft. In their own ways each poet, too, asks searching questions about
what poetry can achieve, and what can be reasonably expected of the
poet him/herself, at the frontier of writing, with 'the imagination pressing back against the pressure of reality'.

Frank Ormsby's *The Darkness of Snow* continues his hit rate of a collection every decade since the 1970s, and embodies the patience and craft
which that implies. The fact that the collection is made up of five sequences
makes more for an interesting structural note than anything else, since
what pervades and unifies all five is Ormsby's attractive sensibility and
dextrous handling of a variety of subjects: he provides most of his own
epigraphs. There is a lovely clarity to the now-seeing of the poet's own
past in the opening sequence, in poems like 'The Cash Railway' and 'The
Gang'; dark humour too, in ones like 'Altar Boy Economics' and the
quasi-allegorical 'Neddy'. He has a countryman's eye for the tiny details
of rural life and its rapidly departing ways. In a poem like 'Rhododendrons',
Ormsby gives an almost prelapsarian quality to the latter as he takes a
good look at what's been lost for modern Ireland's gain: 'Or, as we said,
"rosydanrdums", / never having seen the written word.' Throughout the
first two sequences, there is an easy intimacy with nature, typical of the
generational company he has kept, and the sense of a poet who, having
staked out his patch, is clearly enjoying an already well-honed craft. 'My
Father Again', for example, thrums with tender confidence and absolutely
nails that lingering relationship of the writer son with his dead father:

> I might have been born to write your elegy.
> The moment I lift my pen your soft knock
> will be heard at the door. For fifty years or more
> you have been my work-in-progress.

The second sequence appears to occupy the poet's present-day, as a
retiree contemplating his own mortality and celebrating a new-found
freedom to wander the Waterworks Park, frequent his favourite boozers,

and to enjoy the company of his friends. There are a couple of engaging and affectionate poems dedicated to members of Ormsby's poetic cohort – 'For Ciaran Carson', and 'Lunch in The Crown with Michael Longley' – and a few essays into shorter forms like haiku and tristich, none forced, and all displaying that 'exquisitely refined lyricism' identified by Longley himself.

Throughout, there's an easy approachability to Ormsby's light-handling of subjects and modes made more sonorous by other writers. This is partly down to the ready humour evident in hilarious poems like 'The Cult', and it continues through the latter half of the book, beginning with the ekphrastic sequence, 'Twenty-Six Irish Paintings'. This is a mode that is hard to do well but his versatility and confidence means that we are entertainingly treated to twenty-six ways of Frank looking at a painting. The 'meta-awareness' of his own performative act of looking creates much of the poetry here as it pokes through into poems such as 'Stanley Royle: *The Goose Girl*':

> This neck of the woods
> may be said to be hers in a way it is not mine.
> It begins to be mine as I watch her glide through…

If all this sounds a bit too biddable up to now, then *The Darkness of Snow*'s dark heart beats strongest in two closing sequences which help elevate it to a collection of extraordinary worth. Ormsby's unsentimental self-analysis of the malaise of the Parkinson's Disease that afflicts him links it to Katie Donovan's collection, though there is real humour and affection in these reports from the frontline of his struggle against a disease which recasts him as that mythic Irish archetype, 'Mad Sweeney in the trees'. Ormsby is both nature poet and the poet of nature, chillingly so in the book's superb final sequence, 'The Willow Forest', a fractured narrative of an unnamed tyrant on trial for overseeing the sort of massacre to which we have become depressingly re-accustomed in the past twenty-five years. This is a beautifully nuanced and problematised look at the nature of atrocity, survival, and witness, that forces us to confront the shameful truth that blood alone, does, indeed, appear to move the wheels of history.

Borrowing a phrase from Heaney, Katie Donovan's is an art which often seems to rebuke beauty in favour of truth, breathtakingly so at times. It's been a long while since a collection moved me quite so much and took me upon such a switchback ride from antipathy to admiration and respect. Thomas Hardy famously observed that, 'If way to the better there be, it exacts a full look at the worst', and Donovan's fifth collection is both exact and unstinting in its full look at the personal and domestic worst endured through her husband's agonised struggle against terminal

illness. The pointedly titled *Off Duty* is, then, an entirely worthwhile ad-
dition to the recent sub-genre of cancer chronicles, the steady growth of
which merely reflects the prolonged fade-outs of poets and partners alike,
facilitated by modern medicine. The visceral heft of this collection, however, is derived from its absolute willingness to court dislike at the same
time as it elicits respect. Initially, I found myself alienated and shocked by
the excruciating level of self-regard and an almost autistic want of
empathy for the husband figure, only to realise – under the tutelage of
the poetry itself – that, in recreating that true exclusion of the carer from
the dying sufferer, Donovan is offering us the most honest and heart-
breaking depiction of loss. What the world expects from the Grieving
Wife and what is actually endured by a caring Human Being can be very
different things, the animal inconvenience of which it is poetry's job to
scrutinise. And scrutinise unflinchingly is what Donovan does throughout this book: we are not spared the 'guttural rasp' of the patient's trou-
bled breathing, nor the 'Saucer-sized homunculus' that 'leaks scarlet pus,
stains shirts / emits an overpowering stink', nor – harrowingly – are we
spared the uncomprehending wonder of the two young children who
must witness their father's pain-filled demise. Crucially, we are not spared,
either, every inconvenient or unpalatable truth about the existential
pain-in-the-ass that is being the surviving adult and main carer in such a
situation. And this is *Off Duty*'s main gift to the reader: it problematises
the perceived protocols of a process that is inescapably problematical.

The collection starts buoyantly enough, with a sequence depicting a
world of domestic and maternal bliss, rendered in Donovan's uncluttered
and assured style. The luminous qualities of this opening phase return
somewhat altered towards the end of the collection but, in between,
there creeps a lengthening shadow over the book, commencing with the
poem 'The Next Exit' and the poet's admission that: 'Because you're ill, I
now can't spill / the vitriol the way I did.' Such frank expediency slowly
emerges as the distinctive energy of the book, growing like the cancer it
depicts, defining what follows. Donovan doesn't shy away from sharing
the improper expectations of a wife whose husband's slow and grisly
demise from throat cancer casts him ever more adrift from family and self:

> I'm not ready to be Hallowe'ened,
> I shiver at this Death's Head,
> how its tongue speaks.
> —'HALLOWE'ENED'

As Donovan points out, in 'Retail Therapy': 'This sickness brings the
hero out in him; / in me, the shrew – I have few noble feelings left.'
What works so potently alongside such unwavering frankness is the quiet

accommodation made by a household that includes two young children, whose pathetic witness to their father's loss provides the collection with its most harrowing and heart-stopping moments. Nowhere, for example, is the brutal dehumanisation and alienation of throat cancer more acutely registered than in 'Lips':

> He patrols the corridor,
> pushing the feeding station
> that funnels food up his nostril.
> The sound of wheels on the floor
> is loud in the silence of the children
> huddled behind their mother.
>
> The wheels stop.
> He fondles their heads.
> They do not look up.

This is a harrowing, heart-breaking, and necessary book to which I cannot do justice in a few hundred words. The inevitable happens. Death comes slowly and agonisingly, there is the funeral and the months of numbness before a sort of spring sets in, though it is palliative at best: there is no recovery nor final victory over her husband's death, only a slow assimilation into moments of tenderness and hope figured in their children and the small ongoing details of nature's un-gilded lilies. I can but urge you to read this, weep, and remember that thou, too, art dust.

Eamonn Wall

AN IMMIGRANT RETURNS

The elder's short chin it was
that drew us in. He'd walked
across the street and harked
at us in greeting. His wrinkled
face was warped like weathered
timber ripped from the home's
westward leaning gable. Aged
to outline, seated now amongst
us on our brownish city bench,
we older urbanite idle men like
faint daggers on display. He said
"For many decades I have lived
among foreigners, felt in my heart
famines and bloody wars. I seek
an audience for my tales." An
omnibus had halted at the lights
by a garbage can, two pigeons
wrestled with a candy wrapper.
"I am a native of this place,"
intoned our ghostly interloper.
"The voices have all changed,"
he declaimed, "my old bodega,
lo and behold, flipped to House
of Sushi." A sailor this man
had been, for many decades
flung about from the Maritimes
to Asia's Philippines, Hector
Alvarez, first baseman long ago
for Lincoln H.S.'s winningest
teams. Switching into Spanish,
we joked of a great America
Donald J Trump did not know
and whistled sweet trans-
gressive airs hot off the melting
pot. Even dust blown upward
from the trampled path without
sampling we thankfully inhaled,
Hector's words we brandished
like a hot, newly polished sword.

Beverley Bie Brahic

THE SAND DOLLAR INN

Ocean Views from Every Room

Here, engraved in someone else's
name, is a bench where we can sit
and watch the waves go in and out.
Lean back, sop up the horizontal sun
trawling west across Georgia Strait.
Why don't I leave you here?
Why don't I take a stroll out where
the tide will turn, that wave-stamped
swathe of darker, wetter sand
where families shore up their castle walls
and sift debris for intact shells
faux gems of bottle glass and fossil scraps
of runic worm-written wood
the sea collects for us to hold.

Gerald Dawe

ELEGY
  – Aodán Mac Póilin, 1948-2016

Timorous bird song from the churchyard
where Sarah Hall and her husband, John lie.
Next door the house of the last hangman
displays his trade with a sign of the gibbet tree.
Then on a cold wintry morning
as a bunch of foreign kids check messages
before their day begins,
I hear about your plight, dear friend.

We wouldn't have been up and at it this early,
no question, sea foam would've been flying
over the road, those scornful Sundays,
when the wind battered against windows
and doors and in and out of the draughty
house we rented, heading up the coast
where no one lived on the sea shore,
we managed to 'survive' it all – the 'war' –

without really knowing for how long.
Now your blurred voice and familiar laughter
can't conceal the end of the road –
and how you'd baulk at that, for sure –
head tilted, eyes closed, that's how it was,
'In Praise of the City of Mullingar'
in one place after another, timelessly,
we've been caught out at last.

Patrick Moran

ALMA MATER

Bakey explaining
the college motto,
Hiems transiit

(Winter has passed):
how the repealing
of the Penal Laws

led to the opening
of St. Kieran's,
school and seminary.

⋆

I'd trudge down deserted
corridors, my feet wheezing
on the polished lino;

the walls lined with photos
of ordination groups:
serene, invulnerable.

From somewhere, piano
notes: bursting in my heart,
my vision blurring ...

⋆

And no escaping.
From the shadows, I'd observe
clique after clique

going around the walks.
Emerging into view,
bantering and laughing;

then turning the corner,
their cosy chat receding
beyond my straining ears.

★

Everything closing in.
My days dragging
like a ball and chain.

Grace Wells

FUTURE, PRESENT, PERFECT

Paul Casey, *Virtual Tides* (Salmon Poetry, 2016), €12.
Geraldine Mitchell, *Mountains for Breakfast* (Arlen House, 2017), €13.
Rachael Hegarty, *Flight Paths Over Finglas* (Salmon Poetry, 2017), €12.

Paul Casey's *Virtual Tides* is a vivid blaze of a book, an erudite, zeitgeisty expression of the realities – virtual and otherwise – of twenty-first century Western culture. Here is the 'leaf-free' urban life, the 'world of go-go-go', where 'busy heads control remote bodies', where we have 'for the most part forgotten to breathe', where many of us exist 'out of our minds from fluoride and advertising'. The collection explores a way of living where even gravity has been 'reversed in the top percentile sending rich minds skyward'. A mechanised, industrialised post-modern world that is both 'intimate' and 'oblivious'. The collection is a map of our times, its poems delineate the *now*, plotting our co-ordinates – lost as we are within the labyrinth of technology.

At heart Casey is most interested in the effect all of this is having on us. In his prose piece, 'Ultima Thule', he gives us the delightful and distressing image: 'Some press elevator buttons or traffic-light pedestrian buttons repeatedly, as if these woodpecker urgencies could inoculate them with spirit.' And later he wonders: 'if the children of Spiritus: *inspiratio*; *inspirare*; *inspiracion* – are somehow in a recession of their own'.

What makes all this particularly affective is the way Casey stitches into his portrayal of our Android-regulated world, subtle references and landmark poems that refer back to our earliest phylogenetic experience: stone circles, ring forts, druids, and even our 'chimp' ancestors. Like an extraordinary puppeteer, Casey twitches humanity by the strings, yanking us from our present marinade to dip us back into prehistory, and remind us of our true colours. In the midst of the mechanized world, we stumble on 'A standing stone of city glass', and 'A capstone of progress is washed clean by the sun' ('For Pointing at the Sun'). This is poetry of *spiritual autobiography*, not so much Casey's own story, which comes as a whisper through the collection – but rather humanity's spiritual autobiography, our *collective* experience of the soul's challenge *now*.

Virtual Tides flies on two wings of loss, one beating us forward into an ever more de-sensitised world, the other trailing backwards towards everything we might grieve over before we forget it even existed. We are, he reminds us, living in a world where 'losing touch may soon be de-clared impossible', and '"getting lost" removed from the world database of practical phrases'; and yet, like poet Noel Duffy, Paul Casey is declaring himself a curator of lost things. He writes, 'adieu to the signature, a gesture as personal as the lickable stamp'. Stitched through these remarkable poems is a litany of the precious cultural treasures that are falling extinct in each waking moment: 'talking, now as in decline as incandescent light bulbs'. The poem 'Jack's Orchestra' is an auditory feast of lost sound effects. And 'evolving the hypnic jerk' is a masterful, circumambulatory invocation of losses that returns us right back beneath the human skin to 'the near extinct plantaris, pyramidalis, subclavius, palmaris muscles, from when we fled on all fours and hung out in trees'.

Casey is strong on clever ideas. In 'Defence Force Seeks Artists', he ably melds image and abstraction to convey his idea across the line of polemic into poetry. He's equally successful in 'What the Frack', 'Laughing Lama', and 'Living with Six Lovers'. Throughout the collection he presents us with a heady, acrobatic mix of word and idea, an intensely pleasing display of linguistic gymnastics that juggles and throws us somersaulting mid-air, before he'll once again catch the reader in the safe arms of a steadying, redemptive image, like 'A splinter of sky has pierced the riverbed' ('For Pointing at the Sun'); or a grounded, humane lyric, like 'the last wildflower / on my mind' ('Last Wildflower').

The trouble comes where abstraction and intellect win out over sensation and emotion, and the poems veer toward riddle and puzzle. After Casey's excellent poem 'Virtual Companion', the collection becomes a little arid, a chunk of pages seems to walk you through a desert while your highly intelligent companion talks of things you don't quite understand and the sun gets hotter, your head starting to pound. The small song-bird of emotion flits through this central part of the book branch-hungry, not knowing where to land. But isn't this exactly how it is to live in our radically urbanized, technological world?

One of Casey's great skills is his musicality. Like a Colossus for Cork harbour, he straddles the shores of page and performance with one foot steady in each. This results in urgent rushes of lyrics down the pages of 'Jack's Orchestra', 'monkey's wedding', and 'Bar Beings' – a poem rampant with the letter B – and riffs into a bright, jazz-like yellow in 'Dandelion':

> for milk witch tears in the coffee
> pee-a-bed, wet-a-bed
> dog-piss in the pavement cracks
> the mountain paths

In performance, Casey's poems are tongue-twisters of delight, and on the page his prodigality with language is a political act: he's asking us to not just slow down enough to read, but to be still enough to stay. Casey is ever provocative, and his provocations – however they come – circle the reader back to his theme of the locus of the soul in a world spinning at hyperspeed.

Our virtual tide is perfectly captured in Casey's final poem 'kudzu'. Here, rapidly over-taking technology grows tendrils into the metaphor of Kudzu, the Asian weed taking over the Southern States of America, growing a foot a day. It entwines through the poem, binding us to the *now*, caught as we are in our precarious breath between challenged nature and dominant culture. This is a collection worth having, worth keeping, its torch magnificently illuminates the discomfort of the zeitgeist, and its tongue offers a compelling, effective yawp right back at the times we live in.

Early in *Mountains for Breakfast*, Geraldine Mitchell tells us that 'Wind tangles in rivers of air, catches / on trees, carries sheep bleat, dog bark / – lets them drop', inviting us into the natural world as it is: a Mayo coastline where place, rock, creature, and selfhood intertwine. Mitchell quotes Susan Howe: 'Your words spring from your landscape', and the sentiment is entirely true of Mitchell herself. Landscape and the creatures of place spill from field and shore to comfortably inhabit her lyrics, to speak for her.

Mitchell's poems gift us the connectedness earned from long years living close to nature. The separation between things has blurred. Connection is articulated through language, the verbs of the human realm are given to weather, creatures, trees. Curlews offer instruction, 'Bluebottles bounce // words from room to room'. Starlings prattle, gulls scold. Snow flings 'upstrokes' like a painter. '[T]he sky's a lesson / in geometry'; 'The road runs with / braided water.' Urban delineations exist on the far side of the rain's veil. This is not so much a romanticisation of nature, but merely immersion and inhabitation.

Nothing is adorned, or overwritten, the pacing of Mitchell's images is the slow pace of a walk, the eye falling on one detail and then another. There's sufficient pause, sufficient white space between her sparse images for us to fully absorb the world she presents. Salt air is simply allowed to be, so that we experience it almost first-hand. *Mountains for Breakfast* gives us a direct experience of life on the Mayo coast. Everything is passed on to us as it is. In 'Winter Commons' she writes:

> Mountains for breakfast, the sea
> for tea – there is no other food
> to feast on. We eat winter's yellow
> grass, its blackened branches, moss
> that's fingers deep. We make soup of
> stones, a solitary diet of grey rocks.

In 'Roadkill', Mitchell drags a hare 'by the tip of one long slender ear to the / dignity of grass', and in that one gesture reveals that the whole collection is something of a meditation on dignity. Each of Mitchell's poems speaks in a quiet voice. She is not trying to please, never shows off, won't turn handstands for attention; Mitchell simply writes her clear, lucid lines, and gets on with the work of generously offering the world as it is.

But what begins as a collection articulating the active presence of landscape, soon becomes a narrative concerning the loss of Mitchell's husband to Alzheimer's. From 'Named' onwards there's a departure: 'The sea was tame that afternoon, / the hills radiant and clear.' In 'Conundrum' the poet is presented with 'Spring and a dying mind, / what am I to make of that?' Her days become a place where there's 'no heart for play', where she can only wait and be.

The poems elegantly capture Mitchell's journey between circumstance and trust, half-harboured by the land, carrying on with very little but dignity – and poetry. It is poetry Mitchell fights for again and again, never allowing us to see a dull or clichéd image, so that even as nurses and oxygen come close to the bedside, the poet's eye is still taking us to 'rooks around / the litter bins, portly and severe // as undertakers'. Mitchell is determined to give illness the dignity it deserves. Even in death, bare arms cool 'slow // as stone on a summer night'. The morning of the passing itself becomes a rope; the poet will 'pay it out, pull it in again / until [her] hands chafe'.

Throughout the challenge of her grief, Mitchell protects the reader from experiencing its worst ravages and only exposes us to what is bearable. She remains intensely alone while simultaneously stitched tight to land, creature, weather, and starlight. In 'Wanting', a merlin coming down to snatch the life of a thrush, 'has emptied the garden / of song'. And in the poem 'Grief', that withering emotion 'breaks / on the grace note / of a wren'. There is a gracious restraint throughout, a weave between privacy, disclosure and reveal that lets us walk beside Mitchell in her aloneness, and which ultimately bring us to the following invaluable lines from 'What the Threat of Thunder Does':

> you will always come back
> empty-handed
> to the here and the now
>
> bird song and leaf sway
> the plane tree's marled trunk
> corporeal and dense
>
> and rooted as ever.

The hand that gave the dignity of grass to a dead hare, ultimately gives us the gracious composure of being able to stand empty-handed in the here and now. No greater gift.

Surely a difficult book to write, *Mountains for Breakfast* is nonetheless a luminous read. We can only be grateful that there are such landscapes, such words and writing. Mitchell's nib turns difficult waters into almost halcyon days, offering a calm to winter's storm which ultimately leaves us with 'misted gifts', 'a hoard of sea glass', and the 'indifferent sea' lit by the sun's 'incandescence'. This is a sparse voice at its very best.

Like a new Olympian breaking all former records and taking home several golds, Rachael Hegarty's *Flight Paths Over Finglas* raises the bar on what a debut collection can be. From her first poem, 'Ripples', about her grandmother's life and death, we're exposed to what is simply excellent writing. There is something effortless-seeming about the way Hegarty binds together bewitching language, the most interesting images, perfectly sensuous details, symbols, historical references, soundscapes, distilled lives, and telling gestures like a kiss to a sleeping child, or the lighting of a candle. This is storytelling at its best and the result is a collection of beguiling narratives told in a voice that leaves us hungering for more.

In 'Costume Barracks' she tells the story of Granny Mary born in a British barracks in Athlone, 'Daughter of a Royal Army Lieutenant', who could say nothing to her father about the stonemason's lad she'd met by Magazine Gate.

> ... They courted beyond the town's walls,
>   the streets' gawkers and spiteful talkers.
> A wander by the River Shannon could make a body fall in love,
>   a July swim would have you near drowned in lust
> but a man who could name all the wild flowers on a sunny riverbank —
>   birdsfoot, rush, water avens, ox-eyed daisy and cowslip —
> he's the one who'd have you on the run with ne'er a backward glance.

Linguistically Hegarty is like a chameleon, moving back and forth in time, able to shape-shift the colours and contours of her language to speak in either sepia tones, or modern argot. In 'Tuesdays in Ballymun' her stanzas move seamlessly between the Towers and Akhmatova's Russia – both voices equally authentic and believable. In 'Ancient Guild of Incorporated Brick and Stonelayers' she gives us the clay, soil, and muck of her brick-layer Grandda, and her pre-teen son *'kicking ass for the working class'*.

As the collection moves through its different sections, eras, locations, and characters, each poem opens and spills us into the experience of a vivid world. We lose ourselves into the work, and there's no jolting out of each individual drama, no word in the wrong place, no space for misunderstanding, ambiguity, self-indulgence, or dullness. Although many of the poems gyre around the same place and community, there's no repetition. Each piece offers a slightly different facet of Hegarty, a prism-like poet whose varying narratives are all suffused with her indomitable warrior spirit. Each comes at you, feisty, fighting, delivering you to a forgotten part of your emotional make-up, swimming down into your jaded depths to pull you up by the braces or the underpants, or whatever part of you Hegarty can get her hands on, to shake you out like a doormat into the light, lifeblood and power of poetry.

These participatory poems are likely to sweep up a wide audience, Hegarty is writing about the real challenges ordinary Irish people face, and in so doing she achieves what so many poets fail to achieve: relevance. But she's also at the High Church altar, technically proficient, a priestess of art, craft, and learning. She puts the very best ingredients into her poems, and all the different parts of the reader's brain fire and light up. For those who teach poetry, Hegarty's work offers itself as a new syllabus. What needs to be taught is all here – poems to make any class sit up, the collection a window pouring fresh air into any stifled room. Hegarty has herself been taught at both Trinity and Queen's, her Acknowledgements page is a veritable Who's Who, but what oozes from her poetry is the un-teachable – raw talent, verve, and an inexhaustible ability to clothe grit with iridescent nacre, to make pearl.

What Dickinson did with the dash, Hegarty almost outpaces with the hyphen. A small harvest of these gems produces: 'stone-sore knees', 'cosy-curled', 'gale-fluttered', 'steady-whorled', 'spindly-hungry bones', and the image of herself as a 'tree-shinny-tom-boy'. She's also an audacious master of the grand statement: 'There are things a death cert can't tell you.' 'Maternal death's as dark / as a young family's bereft.' 'Everything that ever was, is and will be, smells of the sea.' 'It's easy to be bold in an observatory. / All you have to do is find the stairs.'

Boldness rears its delicious head through the book, spicing Hegarty's earnest with pure mischief. There's also a generously sprinkled wit that suggests Hegarty won't let herself get po-faced about literature. She'll smoke a joint in Emily Dickinson's garden, and her visits to Thoreau's pond end as only Hegarty could end such a pilgrimage:

> We yield to the cold give
> of cool water between our legs.
> Bask in the tingle of nipples
> breast-stroking lake water.

So many of the poems here, even in their challenges, are songs of praise of one form or another, sung through with fiery compassion, and the result is breathtaking. Rachael Hegarty cannot be recommended enough.

FEATURED POET: STEPHEN SEXTON

Stephen Sexton was born in Belfast, where he is currently finishing his Ph.D. at the Seamus Heaney Centre in Queen's University. In 2017 his poem 'The Curfew' – chosen from a dauntingly large entry – won the UK's National Poetry Competition. In 2014 he published a chapbook called *Oils*, which was the Poetry Book Society Winter Pamphlet Choice. The two previously unpublished poems in this issue continue the themes and tones that are striking in his earlier work.

In his prize-winning poem 'The Curfew' (published in *Poetry Ireland Review* 121), it's possible to look more closely at what these themes and tones are. The poem presents as a bold, adventurous blend of time-frames, disconnected events, political inferences, and personal lyricism. Radicals let animals out of a zoo. They roam around a town. Miners endure their hardships. A grandfather's wisdoms and sayings are remembered. And the fracture of memory and language prevents elegy. There is no effort to connect things, because there is no suggestion they are disconnected. And no wish to explain things, only to illuminate something further with them and, in Stephen Sexton's own eloquent words, 'to create a kind of municipal pastoral scene in which what's happening and what happened are overlaid and integrated'.

In his first poem in this issue, 'Afternoon at the Café Somewhere', it is afternoon in a European city, but the place – never exactly described or defined – constantly slides away from definition. The first line refers to a piazza in 'whatever European city this is'. No one is securely located. No one behaves as we think they should. A man confesses a life crisis, but to a vegetable not to his neighbour: 'yes, he says to the celery / my marriage is over'. The place, the people, the afternoon are fogged in by purposeless gestures; they offer a rich claustrophobia to the reader. And an aphorism sums it all up: 'there is no more joy here / than anywhere else'.

The second poem here, 'Segue', works with surprising twists, swerving in and out of suggestion, with unsettling revelations. The poem opens with a childhood scenario. Boys and frogs – maybe an old and familiar connection there, but the lines that follow darken it: 'The boys who carry ruin in their pockets / are becoming other people.' In the second stanza, time has moved on. The untroubled surfaces of the August day have gone with the boyhood they hosted. Now a man is sitting in traffic. This is years from then the poem tells us, but adds, in a wonderful amendment: 'but cruelty is a time traveller'. And suddenly the segue is revealed.

Stephen Sexton's poems are marked by ambition and invention. His work is distinctive among the poets of his generation for its occasional but sure-footed navigation of the surreal; for its deliberate fractures of time zones and chronologies; and its eloquent, convincing disruptions of the logical and sequential. His writing confirms the welcoming comments in Annie Freud's introduction to *Oils*: 'These are poems to read and re-read. This is a poet to get excited about.'

– Eavan Boland

Stephen Sexton

AFTERNOON AT THE CAFÉ SOMEWHERE

In the piazza of whatever
European city this is
the fourteenth century
white marble arches
do their best to mutiny
against the season

curious breeds of dog
suffer the nuisances
of their genes
lapping the ice water
clement waiters
splash into dishes

and there is no more joy here
than anywhere else.
Espresso cups
clink on their saucers
and the talk in English
is of the portraits

of x and x by so
and so and how once
a mother somewhere
loved that one
of the man standing
waist-deep in a river

his hat a skull
held out in his hand
waving so long
or hello my friend
the current is fine
and I am happy.

The sweet bitter blue smell
of matches
and cigar smoke
is on a breeze
someone prayed
to the gods of weather for

and the Coca Cola
someone said
she'd sell her soul for
is fizzing
in a high ball
on the table.

The rickety waltz
an accordion wheezes
mesmerises no one;
a gypsy jazz
guitarist catching
the likeness

of his father's face
in his own reflection,
drops the beat
and blushes and laughs.
Cousins you imagine
kiss each other

on the cheeks across
the square. A husband
in a bistro sweats,
chiffonades and juliennes
yes, he says to the celery
my marriage is over.

Later the thunderstorm
throws its weight around
and only the statues remain
in the bronze of their poses
dreaming of
the opposite of and.

It will be a long night
says Pierre to the peppermill
in the pale light
the generator rations out,
poaching excellent pears
in honey and moscato:

the masterstroke
of another great banquet
no one living is invited to.
So what he says
to the no one
he loves.

Stephen Sexton

SEGUE

For the boys with the frog this is it.
No one mostly, older girls sometimes
pass on the straggle of back lanes
and it's for the birds what they talk about.
This variety of August
is untroubled surfaces, fields
of barley at the elbow
and within a stroll, a starve
of waste ground fly-tippers rust
their ancient engines on.
A boulder of liver-spotted granite,
a thumbprint on the belly of a frog.
The boys who carry ruin in their pockets
are becoming other people.

Samphire in the copper pan,
a splendour of salmon.
He's in traffic on the bridge
and this is years from then,
but cruelty is a time traveller.
It is paper, cotton, leather, doves,
the slope of Monte Carlo,
chanterelles, the Shangri-Las
the valley of the Rhône,
the Wichita lineman
and its baritone guitar.
A knock at the door, she goes
and a one and a two and a
one two three four.

Darren Morris

ABUNDANCE

It's difficult not to imagine one's marriage as un-improvable.
But after all, we were only pals sometimes. Yet I suppose
nothing of our intimacy would impress you as much as it impressed us.
We taught each other humility and learned loathing on our own.
How must I seem to her, at the edge of fifty and already old,
given to lasting flashes of anger and blindness?
It could be worse, I suppose. With spring such a desert,
we could have spent our boring, perfectly lit Saturdays
not having sex. Or attending birthday parties for other people's children.
We could have been born beneath a different moon, bloodless.
Or ended up as birds, or amoebas, or as a single field of grass.
We could have flown from this slow, particular slaughter.
Never to meet, imagine, nor lived as we did. It's good to keep
a spoonful of repugnance in the throat when having sex
with the same old familiar body. To stay unknowable,
to say uncomfortable things. They say that in our expanding universe,
there are bound to exist our other selves making different choices.
But I pity them, all the rest. Let them burn to dust.
For today you hated my hangover nearly as much as I did.
And still you took me to bed. The sky went green with spartan tornadoes
what ruin none but trailers and barns. But before them – a hail storm.
A shocking, brilliantly white vomitus. A purge of precious stone.
Bouncing. Abounding. Abundance. An impossible purity among
small houses and concrete. A sugaring from the now like a certitude.

Siobhán Campbell

THANKS AND PRAISE

Mark Roper, *Bindweed* (The Dedalus Press, 2017), €12.50.
Louise C Callaghan, *Dreampaths of a Runaway* (Salmon Poetry, 2017), €12.
Iggy McGovern, *The Eyes of Isaac Newton* (The Dedalus Press, 2017), €12.50.

The opening poem, 'Longtailed Tits', sets the tone for one of the moods of Mark Roper's *Bindweed*. Its deft rhythms capture the echo of birdsong, creating aural delight, but the poet also freights this with a sense of more at stake, a metaphorical hinterland where relationships hang 'on every word afraid', and 'you're hurrying after you're calling'. Here is poetry that measures the power of the word seriously, where miscommunication, it's implied, has real consequence. Roper is both a poet attuned to the physicality of the natural world and one who does not eschew the realities of the social world.

While one of this book's presiding moods is that of an open-ended questioning, a kind of quest for an almost-spiritual but elusive moment, the other approach is more definite, giving way to something the poet wants us to know. One of Roper's strengths is to hone in on the object of fascination, working in incremental steps to lay bare both its reality as well as possible symbolic meanings. 'The Wader Cabinet' captures these 'Darners of shoreline', but with their ...

> Careers of risk and rapidity cut short
> they suffer our stare in this cabinet ...

Roper invites us to a particular view of nature in this poem which recognises the need to allow it be no more or less than itself, but which wants to note this as connected to human challenges:

> as if by a closer look we might learn
> how best to let them keep their distance.

This moral stance, rendered with a light touch, pervades this compelling book throughout, and the reader is invited to partake of its hard-won implication.

Roper experiments with form, adopting an aphoristic style of couplet in 'Water and Stone', set in Namibia, and a narrative approach in 'Andean Cocks of the Rock', which uses 'we' to imply a kind of collective experience – something that is tricky to use successfully and which can lead to a slightly declamatory tone. Here, poems set abroad tend to embed the poet's intentions more obviously, making them a little less poetically satisfying than poems that move toward their subject without this kind of filtering.

Part of the second half of the book deals with the long aftermath of a serious mountainside accident. Images of falling and of being buoyed up again meld with recollected moments from being the recipient of care, and in poems like 'Gravity' this transcends recollection and moves towards a controlled elegiac or spiritual epiphany:

> When I fell I knew
> this was not a fall, it was you
> taking hold of me,
> speeding me, rolling me over,
> I felt your grab

Rueful self-awareness permeates this section, and the emotional honesty of the unadorned and exacting stanzas creates a contract of trust with the reader, who is then trained to be ready for insights captured and generated by subsequent pieces, which again emerge from close observation of the natural world. From 'Celandine', which is 'set in a surrender of leaves', to the 'Bee Orchids', Roper's communing spirit uses luminously memorable turns of phrase to find a kind of stay against a darkness quite present to the speaker. As he says of the orchids:

> So grave and so silly.
> They stared me down.

Louise C Callaghan creates beguiling poetry in *Dreampaths of a Runaway* – a mix of lyrics that have something of the gnomic, and more descriptive works capturing lives under various kinds of pressure. Part 1, 'Dreampaths', presents eleven poems with the quality of images re-run cinematically in order to plumb their significance:

> The child reads deeper into the shapes,
> sees over and over, a leaving car.
>   – 'HALLUCINATIONS'

Callaghan is skilful in setting up a situation which seems at first to be enclosed and particular, then opening it out with confident rhythmic purpose. She does this in 'Sea Therapy' where a father and offspring have been skimming stones:

our father

> bends level with the flickered surface
> and trips his stone like a long sentence over the water
> to a faltering three full stops.

In the title poem, the escape from a sleeping household of a child who is perhaps on 'an adventure, some kind of quest', is juxtaposed with the similar running away of the speaker who, looking back, wonders why no one asked 'why?'. There's an authority of vision in the way the poem ends, reaching for larger vistas and implying other worlds of feeling. These are poems that allow the reader room for interpretation. With an ability to create images that are both exact and evocative, Callaghan allows the build-up of these to carry the increasing weight of meaning, resisting any urge to unpack that meaning more fully for a reader.

At the same time, there's a clear presence of the poet herself, humanist in intention, empathetic – but clear eyed. In the twelve lines of 'Memory and Grief', she manages big themes of inherited trauma with acute observation and restraint by focusing on a story told about amnesia after a horse-riding fall:

> the blameless mare, grazing on wood-sorrel,
> bridle hanging loosely on her neck,
> nickering softly as he came to.

The 'coming to' implied is clinched by the final stanza, which reveals a background both of terrible loss and of mental illness, 'never spoke' about.

Part 2 contemplates different forms of the 'Daily Practice' of its title, invoking artist-mystic Agnes Martin ('Blake, without angels') and dedicating a number of elegies to poets and writers. The poem that gives this section its title is a striking work, taking on how a family enable a loved one to die a good death. This work does not flinch from what is actually occurring: 'And now she has gone beyond / personality'. It renders both how family members react differently and how private grief can be, even when surrounded by others. What makes it memorable though is the control in the short-line stanzas and turns of phrase which burrow into the reading mind:

> in and out – her faltering mother-breath –
> that no names, no words can follow.

Callaghan uses an almost classical inflection in many poems, dipping in and out of iambic metre. She makes good use of the present tense in

POETRY IRELAND REVIEW 123 | 93

poems including 'The Copper Beach at the Main Public Library', and this
suits her visual imagination, unfolding images and scenes for the reader.
The book ends with a series of poems concentrating on the life and
work of Francisco de Goya. Here the poet combines observations on the
machinations of power with a keenly felt meditation on the role of an artist in society. The ending of 'Happy Birthday' – 'Mercifully, no conclusion'
– could be a coda for this collection, with its generous capaciousness and
sense of understated wisdom throughout.

If Roper and Callaghan speak in a mainly straightforward manner, the
voice in Iggy McGovern's *The Eyes of Isaac Newton* can be both tongue-in-
cheek and archly knowing, self-deprecating and deadly serious – sometimes
within the one poem. Coupled with this tonal play is an ability to give the
sonnet and other forms real purchase for our contemporary moment by
combining a delight in formal constraint with a wit that simultaneously
mocks the poet for such attempts. The extended conceit on eyes and
eyesight which permeates the book draws attention to the multi-layered
approach of the poet to ideas of perception, beginning with the very first
piece, 'Hypermetropia', with its story of a Dublin Tommy and his unsuit-
able glass eye.

This is poetry which interrogates its own artifice even as it implies an
underlying wish for that artifice to satisfy. 'Alliteration' tells a domestic
story that has a larger hinterland, in a tight sonnet that pits 'Fuckin' Fenian'
against 'Gang Green', and the 'at least till the fighting is over' of 'Civilian'
marks one of the darker undertows of the work – related to Ireland's
'Troubles', but also to wider concerns. The combination of scientific fact
with a kind of forensic ability to hone in on self-delusion leads to a number
of poems which end before they might have in another poet's hands. This
means that the reader has to work that bit harder and at times become
implicated more explicitly, as in 'Radio':

> No, none of you got this one
> but isn't that all part of the fun?

McGovern is a modernist in this regard – he draws attention to the con-
struction of the work in order to ensure a reader is not lulled into false
senses of poetic security, and then he laughs with us too:

> Call us if you find that sordid;
> this programme was pre-recorded.

There are occasional moments when the serious intent behind the work
is glimpsed. In a poem in three parts called 'Love', we encounter several
moods. The first section, 'The Request', is the 'Write me a real love poem'
request of an ever-loving wife:

not one of your trademark ironies;
from the heart this time, not the head.

But a natural restraint and what almost feels like a fear of embarrassment on the speaker's part leads to acknowledging the difficulty of meeting the request by also pushing the poem further in sections 2 and 3. 'Parodies Lost', the middle section, is a tour de force of parodic delight, borrowing from everyone from Dickinson to Bishop but somehow also managing to reflect upon the subject of the dedication, the poet Dennis O'Driscoll, whose books of quotations from poets were both jokingly reverent and irreverent. This work provides more than one way to read it on the page, since the second lines of each couplet add up to a separate story, anchored by the slightly doleful 'I lost the chance to score when dispossessed'. It takes a half-line at the end, 'Soccer is a bit like Poetry, it's a funny old game', to more fully imply the emotion which otherwise is deftly kept just outside the poem's workings.

The third and final section of 'Love', 'Leaving the Golden Hind' makes another move. Ostensibly referencing the ship of Sir Francis Drake, these three quatrains are infused with human-sized moments of the 'us' in question who are 'afraid / to wash away all the good luck' in what is perhaps the speaker's attempt to answer the first request. That this love poem becomes a contemplation of the difficulties of expressing love is testament to the control of the poet, who finds off-beat and striking ways to show a reader how it feels to be 'masking the drip / from a thousand tiny cuts'. Perhaps this poem is also referencing the difficulty of capture of the Golden Hind of Artemis – in the guise of the Herculean task of poetry-making. On the evidence of *The Eyes of Isaac Newton*, Iggy McGovern is more than up to that task and he might even find a way to 'risk collapse of this dark firmament' – from 'Pupil' – slightly more often, as indeed, the import of the wife's request in 'Love' may actually imply.

These three arresting collections are all well served by their publishers, with Roper and McGovern under the Dedalus Press imprint and Callaghan coming from Salmon Poetry. The artwork used by the publishers' designers adds to the pleasure of reading the books, with an illustration by Aislinn Adams on *Bindweed* and a painting by Goya on *Dreampaths of a Runaway*. Production values are excellent, and readers and poets are clearly well served by the dedicated professionals within the Irish poetry publishing scene – thanks to them all.

Lani O'Hanlon

TOUCHED

Last night it woke me, a thimble of light cutting
through the slit in the curtain, on your side of the bed.

You slept on, unaware of its still nesting
like the white sea glass we found on Curragh strand.

But it must have affected you all the same;

two hares rose up in the field beyond,
a vixen cried out, her throat full of moon.

I touched the silver thumbprint on the back of your head.

Elizabeth O'Connell-Thompson

REVERENCE

Now that it is too late to lose anything but sleep,
        I picture you zoetroping though fence slats,
                your movements broken, ceaseless.

I miss nothing of that life but the shuddering
        sound of horses as they climbed the hill nightly,
                their breath a puff of frost on our window.

Living in the city means I cannot trace
        the clucking of chickens to any neighbor's yard,
                but the rooster's crow beats the morning smooth.

I am unsure of where they came from,
        these visions streamed with light,
                if not the palsied hands of the good Lord himself.

Final line from AJ Kinsel's commentary on 'Jolene (33 R.P.M.)',
on the blog *Something About Blacktop*.

John Liddy

Who is that man beating a woman
in front of two frightened children?
Her face a bloody mess, the man
indifferent to our bidding.
What can we do to disentangle
such a scene in a park
on an evening's ramble?

Hold him until the police come,
only to be released because no
charges are brought by the victim?
What can we do for that battered
woman and the scars of her offspring
which open like freshly planted
flowers again and again?

Keith Payne

A SUBURBAN SUNDAY
  – after Paula Meehan

We never talked about hunger strikes
in our house. Back home after the pub –
Sunday Times crossword done while your man
twirled around the tables with issues
of *An Phoblacht* held up to his chest;
you'd buy one, leave it on the table
and later varnish over the fact.
I'd eyes only for orange Fanta,
that unicorn and your cold, black pint.

Stiofán Ó Briain

Mór an t-ionadh orm,
tú a fheiceáil anseo,
chomh beo 'is a bhíonn tú
i nduibheagáin mo chuimhne.

Is ait liom do ghruaig nua
agus an fáinne ar do mhéar.
Bhí tú Tú i m'intinn;
'nois is beag m'aithne ort.

An fhorbairt thruallaithe
a mhilleann an íomhá,
a phléascann bearna
idir tusa agus mo Thusa.

Tá a gáire agat, 'is a súile,
tá a nathanna is a fuinneamh,
ach tá an craiceann rógheal.
Insíonn dath do bheol bréag.

Cad a rinne tú le mo Thusa?
Cár chuir tú spéirbhean mo chuimhne?
Ar fhuadaigh, ar scanraigh, ar mharaigh
tú bean bheo dhaingean m'aigne?

Luíonn a seanshúile ar mo mhéar;
ag fiosrú fhianaise m'fhorbartha.
Pléascann tú le bréagmheidhir cheiliúrtha;
ag caoineadh bhás do Mhise.

Ag dul i mbun ath-aithne lena chéile.
Ag glanadh cuimhne le nua-thaithí.
Ag fuadach, ag scanrú, ag marú
na Sinne a chruthaíomar.

Fágaim slán leat a nuaThusa.
Go dtaga rath ar do shaol.
'Is ar shaol na mílte thusa
a chasfaidh ar na mílte Mhé.

Mary Gilliland

LUCKY NUMBER

7 8 9   1 2 3
lasso of infinity

spring stalled, the buds like eardrums
waiting for the work to work in me

you have a headache, you cannot sleep
you want the sun out and gone

a yellowed yellow pad
the loose unpretty heart

Maitreyabandhu

ROGER FRY AT LANGHAM PLACE

'A man of profound sensibility but exacting honesty'
was how Virginia Woolf described him – ascetical,
standing in evening dress silhouetted by the slides
he called for, lifting his pointing stick, discoursing
on Rembrandt, Chardin, Poussin, a roll call
of wonders, and somehow, she tells us, seeing them
afresh, pausing and pondering, betraying his
fastidiousness, calling for the next slide, gazing
through his glasses, rethinking, refiguring apostles
and cherries, the funeral of Phocion, till finally
calling for a late Cézanne, then stopping again, looking
again (the audience hushed, looking at him looking,
raising his stick but stopping, baffled), he shakes
his head and rests his stick on the floor. It went, he said,
beyond any analysis of which he was capable.
And so instead of saying 'Next slide', he bowed,
and the audience emptied into Langham Place.

Erin Halliday

INGLIS & CO. LTD.

The streets would be black as bread ovens when my grandfather left for work,
the wet flagstones mirrored like glassy oysters underfoot.
The house lulled and purring in wool, flannelette and flock,
he'd step onto Picardy, street lights burnishing the Cregagh route.

Woodstock, over the Lagan, to Eliza Street, cobblestones like ostrich eggs underfoot –
or the Belfast Baps he'd watch belted along, ceiling height, with their rock-hard crust.
He'd pass the 'day men' at the gates, faces burnished by the bakery light, resolute,
then on with his whites – one of the tabernacle: Aspinal, Ferris, Halliday, McCluskey.

Sweet Veda, the powdery Farmhouse, Lodger's barrel, and Cottage loaf with its
    garland crust,
the roast and sugared smells climbing the steps to the Bread Department; malty, hot –
millers' alchemy: Dennis, Bob, and Jimmy, white-shirted, thumbing the flour,
    breathing yeast.
The milky heat would rise, brimming, stretch spongey hours on the languid clock.

At home, he'd still hear the kneading gears, smell the toasting loaves, watch the clock,
till, 'piece' in his pocket, he'd snib the door on the house's purring kitchen in the dark –
from the languid warmth of bedsheets, to his hours in Inglis' buttery heat;
the streets were black as the bread ovens when my grandfather would leave for work.

Gerard Smyth

REMEMBERING GERARD FANNING (1952–2017)

My first sighting of a Gerard Fanning poem was in an issue of the old UCD literary journal, *St Stephens*, in 1970. The young poet, then a student at the college, would have been eighteen, the age at which it is never quite certain whether the novice is in it for the long haul, or simply going to opt out, or fade away. He did, of course, endure, and almost by stealth built up his body of work, forging a distinctive style that is striking for its originality. Poetry became a vocational part of his life, and he earned a place as an exceptional exponent of the art, as well as one of its most dedicated advocates and supporters.

It was evident from his first collection, *Easter Snow* (The Dedalus Press, 1992), that he had developed his own beguiling tone and aesthetic, a quite unique poetry of sometimes compelling strangeness. It seemed to come from marginal zones, in 'the dark of Ireland's holiest hour' and 'the lull of mid-evening'. It is a poetry that powerfully conveys dreamlike sensations and moods, often suffused with a melancholy beauty.

His imagination was informed by a range of cultural interests that finds its way into and through his poems: the movies of John Ford and Fellini, among other film-makers; McGowran's and McGovern's takes on Beckett; the jazz of Bud Powell and Dexter Gordon; the Laytown races; Boss Croker; and Lucia Popp. Even his shortest poems contained so much, and in a matter of a few lines could swing from 'St Patrick's Day in Bologna' to 'the monastic settlement of Skellig Rock'.

Like his fellow poetry addict Dennis O'Driscoll, his day job was working for the government (the title of his second collection). Like Dennis, he recognised and trusted the merits of the office routine as a counterbalance to the solitary task at the poetry desk. Poetry allowed him to 'rewrite the cloven, haphazard / Labyrinth of the order of [his] life'.

In his four collections, and an as-yet unpublished fifth book, *Rookery*, his daring imagination offered surprising and sometimes off-beat perspectives. A kind of Beckettian humour, too, lurks here and there, as in this, from the title poem of *Rookery*:

> I've always loved the elevator,
> the way it comes when you call.
> And I disdain that cardiovascular fad
>
> of taking the stairs ...

The subject of poetry – and poets – fuelled most of the conversations we had over many years of friendship. His conviction about the value of good poetry was profound, yet he was modest and self-effacing when it came to his own talents. If there had been a school of 'laid-back' poets, Gerry would have been Head Boy. There was no vaunting ambition; he just got on with it.

In his poem 'A Cycle On Bettystown Strand, he alludes to 'quiet hearts'. So many of us, and none more than his beloved wife Bríd, will miss Gerry's own quiet gentleness. He leaves behind not just a lifetime of poetry, but a lifetime of heroic fortitude in the face of testing health issues since a young age. While poetry became a life-sustaining force, his own Zen-like temperament and disposition, his humane outlook and cultured mind, all added to his strengths and to his personality. He was well-armed with a true sense of the important things.

A QUIET HEART
in memory of Gerard Fanning

I was out of town when you needed back-up
(like Earp at the *OK Corral*).
So our last farewell was under the sign
for Finn's Hotel, where your hand held high
gave a valedictory salute.

We sauntered off on separate journeys –
you as far as the sea-coast villas,
I to see images by Vermeer. Our last toast
was to the poets we trust – two coffee cups
served to us by a girl who spoke French words.

The news you had was matter-of-fact.
It came direct from your quiet heart –
as quiet as the footfalls
of *The Man Who Shot Liberty Valance*,
the apples that fall on September grass.

– Gerard Smyth

Colin Graham

LEAVINGS

Deryn Rees-Jones, *What It's Like To Be Alive: Selected Poems* (Seren Books, 2016), £12.99.
Colette Bryce, *Selected Poems* (Picador Poetry, 2017), £14.99.

Deryn Rees-Jones's *What It's Like To Be Alive* begins with 'The Great Mutando' who 'Pulls rabbits out of hats / ties up the day with handker-chiefs in silk'. The Great Mutando's skills, his ability to knot handkerchiefs in secret places or make a dog from balloons, seem to be an easy meta-phor for the poet as maker, magician, puller-off of linguistic tricks. Rees-Jones initially offers Mutando as an aspirational model, but in the midst of her poem tempers the effect. Of Mutando's six hidden doves, 'Five fly, one suffocates. / A little drop of shit / / runs down his sleeve'. Mutando's incapacities define him as much his skills. The undercutting of metaphors of airy possibility with a reality that is more viscerally compelling than the flight of fancy it punctures is a perfect start to this 'Selected Poems', beginning with poems from *The Memory Tray* (1994) and ending with a new elegy, 'I.M.'.

The title poem from *The Memory Tray*, included here, gives a strong sense of Rees-Jones's early work – the language is direct, controlled, persuasive, and yet inquisitive. 'The Memory Tray' is a conceit on the parlour game, an extended metaphor circulating around the things and voices that memories are hinged on to, and which ends with an amalgam of a list and an ironic act of catalogue of the untameable memories which are dreams. As with 'The Great Mutando' there is an underlying desire here to lift the weight of the material world out of its ordinary gravita-tional pull. 'Blue', an unusually free-wheeling poem, slipping in and out of references to American poets and inhabiting their voices, is a joyful act of memory which also feels like a preparation, a poetic voice testing its possibilities and realising its capacities.

Rees-Jones extends the strength of the voice she develops in *The Memory Tray* in subsequent volumes, particularly in her exploration of how sensuality, sexuality, and love can deepen a sense of both the life lived and the poem written. Poems in this 'Selected' from *Signs Round a Dead Body* (1998) show how Rees-Jones shifts towards eroticism as a way to invoke a stronger, more *affective* sense of a worldly reality, as if the magic of Mutando was something of a dead-end, a strategy with no place to go. This turn to the body and sensuality does not attempt to elevate the worldly beyond itself but instead intensifies perception and the phenomenological evidence of being-in-the-world. The sequence 'Song of Despair', written in a sparse and distilled verse, is by turns affirmative and tentative about love, and, in its fifth section, epitomises Rees-Jones's sense that the (erotic) body may be the actual and metaphoric site of meaning:

> So I raised you from the dead.
> So I washed you, licked your armpits, the soles of your feet, untangled
> the spidery lines of your matted hair,
> picked leaves and insects from your well-shaped limbs,
> blew life into your mouth
> and sang to you.
> So I suckled, promised, fed and enfolded you.
> So I hated, loved, scorned even myself,
> was tenderness, a body to you.

The lover's body and the persona's own here are hardly idealised – it is their palpability and corporeality that is the foundation for the resonance they have. When the persona says she 'blew life into your mouth', it is exactly this possibility (that one comes properly and fully alive in the bodily presence of another, and that this being alive gives consequence to everything else) that the poem moves towards – not transcendence, but somatic intensity.

Rees-Jones's *Quiver* (2004) is a clever amalgam of her previous modes of poetic voice with a murder mystery narrative – inventive, funny, gorgeously confusing, it picks up on traits within the genre and detaches them from narrative logic. ('Clone', in style, dedication ['after PM'], and – tongue-in-cheek – in title, recognises the volume's similarity to the narrative poems of Paul Muldoon).

What It's Like To Be Alive culminates in poems from *Burying the Wren* (2012), a raw, piercing volume trying to comprehend the death of her husband from cancer. In poems such as the fractured sonnet 'After You Died', grief and absence are confronted full-on; the moon, once a metaphor of the flightiness of romance, is now 'there, her face full with a fierce singing'. And this poem ends with a hint of rhyme ('cohabiting' with 'singing') and disquiet:

> And the dark again became a place
> of sleep, a wild thing cohabiting.

It takes not only strength of character and thought but a strength of poetic voice to enter into grief in poetry and to channel the chaos of the overwhelming forces of loss into poetic form. In *Burying the Wren* Rees-Jones shows an extraordinary ability to comprehend her own mourning with utter self-awareness and lack of emotional compromise. *What It's Like To Be Alive* ends with a previously unpublished poem, 'I.M.' which revisits the grief of *Burying the Wren* in a more reflective way, in a sequence of systematically controlled poems – each is thirteen lines long, as if she were still not quite ready to write complete sonnets. *What It's Like To Be Alive* is a chance to reflect on the depth of Rees-Jones's poetry to this point, and to see the growth of a fierce poetic intelligence.

Colette Bryce's *Selected Poems* covers four full volumes and two shorter collections, beginning with *The Heel of Bernadette* (2000), and thus functions as a kind of 'mid-career' selected, much like Rees-Jones's *What It's Like To Be Alive*. Bryce's poetry is taut and economical, tending to use regular and repeated stanzaic form and patterns of rhyme and half-rhyme which allow it to pitch its thought through and against the restraint of such formality. Bryce's childhood Derry is a touchstone in her work, though not in a sentimental or mawkish way. Even more than most towns and cities in Ireland, Derry has been memorialised in cheesy songs – in her poem 'Derry', Bryce exorcises the lyric ghost of Phil Coulter:

> I was born between the Creggan and the Bogside
>   to the sounds of crowds and smashing glass,
> by the River Foyle with its suicides and rip tides.
>   I thought that city was nothing less
>
> than the whole and rain-domed universe.

Bryce is both parodying the Coulter-ish tear in the eye and taking possession of that emotion. Her poem remembers Derry in its politics and its social realities, while also knowing that its very existence as a poem is part of its separation from those realities. She and her sisters all leave Derry for third-level education 'across the water': 'armed with a grant from the government / – the Butler system's final flowers' (referring to the Butler Education Act and its legislation giving fees and subsistence grants for university education). The poem ends when the time comes for Bryce, or the poem's first-person voice, to leave, and the poem turns back on itself its own certainty about what Derry is:

> I watched that place grow small before
> the plane ascended through the cloud
>   and I could not see it clearly any more.

The literal separation from childhood here becomes a kind of metaphysical trait in Bryce's way of seeing the world – a constant play between individuality and rootedness, detachment and attachment. Her poem 'The Republicans', in simple, descriptive mode, sets the utter ordinariness of ex-IRA men against an unspoken sense of what these men are expected to be like in peacetime Northern Ireland, and thus seeks, quietly, for some way to understand the ideological forces which underpin the banalities of the poem. (The poems here from *The Observations of Aleksandr Svetlov*, from 2007, hint at a similar interest in the afterlife of ideology within post-communism).

As the flight image at the end of 'Derry' suggests, Bryce's poetry is not limited to or by its Irish contexts. It constantly separates and returns to Ireland via self-conscious processes of disengagement, and this exilic sensibility, half-in, half-out, may be reflected in some of Bryce's less clearly 'Irish' poems, and in her deployment of literary techniques. 'The Pines', for example, is a beautifully crafted piece – a lightly metaphoric poem in which the trees are anthropomorphised and imagined as both singularly individual and simultaneously collective, in need of each other's company:

> Each is born
> to bow and die
> but one will tilt,
> from time to time,
> awkwardly
> to another's arms

This tentative connection is made in the sounds of the poem when the following stanza rhymes 'Lovers' with 'keepers' and echoes the 's' sounds of 'insomniacs' with 'secret hours' two lines later. Here, as elsewhere, Bryce's poetry uses a range of types of rhyme (full, half-, internal, vowel) to consider the correspondences between things, and their interconnections.

'Belfast Waking, 6 a.m' plays on a kind of half-insomniac watchfulness which recurs in several poems. Here the formality is loosened but not gone, so that the stanzas vary from three to six lines and leftovers of rhyme are everywhere apparent. Or rather, this being a dawn poem, they have not yet happened. Nothing in the poem, at this indistinct hour of the day, has quite found its heft or its centre, as the maintenance man who does early morning repairs on the 'the city's empty confessionals' (the telephone boxes, 'out of place/in the cool new century'), seems to put the mechanics of the city's waking hours in process. The foxes and cats, the bin lorry, the footsteps and cleared throats of pre-dawn time all presage the 'moment, precise/when the streetlamps of Belfast / quietly go out, a unanimous decision, / ... / at the advent of the ordinary / business of the day'.

Along with its contemplation of connections and failures to connect, of history and its potential to enable or to trap the individual, the kind of spiritual celebration of the rituals of secular ordinariness which happens in 'Belfast Waking, 6 a.m.' is what characterises the strength and integrity of much of this selected edition of Colette Bryce's poetry.

Joseph Woods

DRIVING TO DELVIN
  – i.m. R Dardis Clarke (1939 – 2013)

> I came to where the road from Laracor leads
>   – FR Higgins

Having left Higginsbrook house and earlier
having paid my respects at the poet's grave

at Laracor – how swiftly he followed
his adored Yeats – and recalling

from the family archive and cuttings
the great and good who made it

to his funeral on that January morning
during the Emergency and forever in black

and white, the frost-burnt fields
and empty white road snaking from Dublin.

And now dear Dardis Clarke whose father
Austin, was one of those assembled that day,

and of course Dardis's odd devotion
to Higgins which took many forms

and included twenty years ago,
his pilgrimage to the grave,

found under a yew tree as he predicted
and the poet prophesied.

And exceptionally for him,
leaving Dublin behind for a day,

always at two with nature
and never learned to drive nor needed to.

Now he's gone too, a genial Karl Marx
always hatted and clad in black,

to become the airborne dust of his beloved city.
I turned onto a road, saw a sign for Athboy

and with a rare half-day to squander
knew I must drive in that direction

if only toward an impulse from childhood.
Cloud maps billowing, streaks of blue,

barely enough for a sailor's trousers,
verges bursting full of hemlock

or devil's bread as we knew it
and the luminous greens and browns

of trees in the midlands at the beginning
of a summer that would break all records,

and one in which I was leaving,
that old restlessness, and again for the East

only this time with family.
Soon, the half-remembered trajectory,

that old route from Drogheda to Greenhall,
darkest Longford and its curious isolation

by its being in the centre and close
to the mysterious turlough, a vanishing lake

that filled, flooded and was drained by the Shannon
and swallowed as a child, my mother's sister,

whom I still think of as a third aunt.
And the third man? My father back then in his Wolseley,

who claimed he could have done the journey
in his sleep and did once, ending up perched

above a ditch, wheels churning air. Blessedly
on his own, he brushed himself off,

and carried along 'plain sailing'. Fortnightly forays
with never an overnight, except in summer,

a pull towards my mother's midlands sadness
magnet back when grandparents,

and even parents were all alive. I'd announce
to them if I could, that finally at forty-six,

I'm driving if not quite legally
and I can almost hear whispers in my ear,

'go and do the test like a good gosson'.
As if qualified to drive you're admitted

to the human race, which is true
for this country. How twisted these roads

still are, which only now explains
that early lifetime of car sickness

and our family method of curing it;
walking ahead of the stopped car

until the motion had worn off
and the head slowly steadied.

You waved back when you were ready,
the car slowly catching up as you faced

into a few more miles of baked leather
upholstery and benign cigarette smoke.

My parents' patience still stays and how
there was never a hurry if you were poorly.

At Athboy, I glimpse McElhinney's
Department Store, another midland

incongruity from childhood, *Why go to Dublin
for a wedding outfit when you can go to Athboy?*

and since no easy parking space, another sign
carries me along, this time for Delvin,

the road dishing out its own reminders.
Only then, I recall the crash

leaving Delvin; an L-shaped turn
at the bottom of the hill that almost

took us to oblivion. Tom flitting me
from Mullingar, before Japan

and he soon after for the Middle East.
A short high-speed slide through rain

and into a wall, the car sizzled like
a big steak flung on a pan and steam rose

as water on coals. Prone, seat-belt lacerated
I asked him to cast over me,

feeling my insides might be out.
He lowered me onto the wet verge.

Only then, remembered the brown Winchester
in the back seat, swaddled in sweaters.

A bomb of pure alcohol, which I'd brought
from the laboratory, tired of accounting for it

to Customs inspections,
thought I'd wipe the sheet white,

packed it for home as a preservative,
unaware my dissecting days were already over.

It would niggle me for years,
sat in a shed so close to my parents' house,

threatening their peace. Worrying
at a distance and sometimes

dreaming of winter sun igniting it
until I called my father to finish with it.

In Casualty that night, the doctor advised
against air travel with a depressed lung;

I was gone within the week
and Tom soon afterwards

with a promise he'd see me in Kyoto.
Never to see home again, a brawl in a bar

in Bahrain undid him and sound sleep
from which there would be no awakening.

I searched for something of him
on the internet but found nothing,

a few photos stored and one in the head,
him grinning outside Carberry's pub,

with a sneaky daytime pint,
a half-life stilled in sunshine.

The L-shaped bend has been smoothed out
and my car ambles up the hill

to the main street, the Greyhound Bar & Lounge,
Powers Whiskey on its gable and from where I think,

Tom might have phoned from that night.
Once I stood across from that bar, facing down

the hill, hitching home, cross-country
when a child appeared and without

as much as a Mexican standoff, cast a stone at me.
I royally cursed the town and crassly invoked,

to myself, its book burning episode,
a slight never quite shaken off,

of that oddly personified title,
The Valley of the Squinting Windows

And strange to recall its author
was at the funeral at Laracor,

old pals and close. Not so his father,
the local teacher, forced to emigrate

for his son's indiscretion and the catastrophe
of a writer in the family.

Call it one-horse, but this town sits
so vivid from childhood

and simply passing through;
the Medical Hall with its quartz relief

of a mortar and pestle now sells wedding dresses.
I peer into the interior of a bar,

dressed in Formica, that's long since closed,
walk the length of the town like pacing

a long platform where a rattling horsebox
does for a train. Taking in the gaps

between buildings which open to hay sheds
and paddocks, a kind of Wild West façade;

a row of buildings then prairie beyond.
And what has happened here in over twenty years?

Unfair of me to freight its one street
with past collisions and yet I'm trying to lay

something down, a store to set by,
for the long haul back East.

Start by driving in that direction,
the downward hill, the erased

'Accident Black Spot'
the now straightened bend

leaving behind a world contained
and lives you hardly knew existed.

Michelle O'Sullivan

BLUE FOR A WONDER

i.
I lie in the shadow of the tree at the front of the house.
The new grass that touches my shoulder is spider-soft.
A 4pm sun scattershots the hedgerow of lilacs.

Birdsong finds me in clues and snippets. And disappears
unresolved. A glimpsed at peaceable sense –
hinds detected, maybe grazing.

ii.
The neighbour's roses have been abandoned
for another year. Guiltless, I cut long stems of those
I favour and bring an armful of their rednesses home.

Sometimes I imagine a tap running, or a woman
admiring the suddenness of a sun-darkened room;
I know those spaces haven't been lived in for years.

iii.
An older threshold. And the repeated study
of the outside bright. Minutes pass
before a reflection is visible.

Like an animal that's become aware,
it disappears when I go to touch.
My hand rests in that dark.

NINE QUESTIONS FOR MICHAEL LONGLEY

Belfast poets Stephen Sexton and Stephen Connolly posed the questions. And Belfast poet Michael Longley answered them.

October saw the publication of Sidelines: Selected Prose 1962–2015. *You speak of your admiration for certain painters and musicians. Has your appreciation of these arts always been that of an observer? Were you around painting or music as a child?*

Eight years my senior, my sister Wendy could have been a good pianist but didn't follow it through. Her flawed playing of Chopin and Schumann was soul-music to me as a boy. When I was fifteen or so I laboriously transferred from her sheet music onto the yellowing keyboard, note by note, a couple of the easier Chopin preludes. It took me months of fumbling. I desperately wanted to get inside music. I listen to music every day, classical music and jazz. It is a huge part of my life. Towards the end of his life my father took to painting landscapes. They weren't much good, but it matters to me that he felt the urge. Friendship with painters has been a blessing over the years, going right the way back to the Sixties. Every few years I write a catalogue note for a fellow spirit. I have included some of this art criticism in *Sidelines*. I am very proud of my daughter Sarah's passionate work. On the cover of *Sidelines* her portrait of me in the Carrigskeewaun cottage seems to encapsulate the whole book.

Have you ever written prose fiction?

No. My mind doesn't work that way (although I hear the sound of poetry in the prose of, say, Sebastian Barry and John Banville).

Some of the first jazz records celebrate their 100-year anniversary this year. The facility to record music in this way, and offer it to the future, undoubtedly changed the way popular music was consumed and produced. Have 'advances' in technology changed the way you write?

Yes, the three minutes of the old 78 rpm gramophone record obliged the early jazz geniuses to organise their thoughts and make eloquent use of every second. That's still a good model for writing poetry. I am no electronic whizz-kid, but I now find it difficult to think without my computer. The big danger is the specious authority the machine can lend to garbage – as with meaningless spatial arrangements or when words have a line pretentiously struck through them. Poetry primarily has to be heard rather than seen.

When you are spoken of as a political poet, it's often for those poems addressing the history of violence in Northern Ireland, and the World Wars. Your pastorals and poems of landscape may not be typically thought of as political poems, but to preserve a natural image in the way that you do is a political act. It seems like you're engaged in a sort of conservationism, a kind of aesthetic ecology. Do you see these poems in this way?

In a way all poems are political. Poetry itself is a kind of conservation. Poetry gives things a second chance. Perhaps my most political poems are concerned with how we treat the plants and the other animals. They are at our mercy. The planet is at our mercy. I believe that a poet's imagination should be like Noah's ark with room for all the animals. I believe that we shall die if we let the wild flowers die.

Kate Kellaway has said in her review of The Stairwell, *that in those poems, 'Birth and death are never far apart.' Derrida says that, 'in calling or naming someone while he is alive, we know that his name can survive him and already survives him'. Listing and the naming of specific flora and fauna are notable features of your work. Do you see any connection between listing, naming, and the elegiac impulse?*

At services here in memory of victims of the Troubles and, in America, at 9/11 commemorations, the soul of each occasion is the enumeration of the names of the dead, a litany that reverberates like a prayer. Edwin Lutyens's great Thiepval Arch in Picardy is dedicated to 'The Missing of the Somme'. On its walls are carved the names of the 73,000 men whose bodies were never identified. In Washington, visitors to the Vietnam memorial lovingly touch the engraved names and slip messages and flowers between the great black slabs. In Berlin, at the Memorial to the Murdered Jews of Europe, the names and professions of the victims of the Holocaust are recited, one by one, on a screen. It will take years to mention everyone, but it matters desperately that everyone is mentioned. The names are all we have. We have no choice but to carve them into stone.

You have been rightly praised for the clarity and precision of your language. Language's relationship to 'truth' has always been kind of slippery, but in politics – domestic and international – it seems the current climate of mistruth and disinformation exploits that relationship even further. Plato might have wanted to run poets out of town. Is the writing and reading of poetry any more or less useful than it has always been?

I have said a few times that poetry is the opposite of propaganda. Poetry is language at its most complex, subtle and concentrated. It encourages us to question church and state, and to think and feel for ourselves as clearly and honestly as we can manage. Poetry exposes such death-dealing lies as 'the final solution to the Jewish problem', 'collateral damage', 'ethnic cleansing'. Just now, the most powerful man in the world has a banal mind and a limited vocabulary. So the value of poetry is blazingly obvious. What use it can be is harder to discern.

'Something happened in the Sixties', you've said. Have you, even now, any explanation for the particular flourishing of poetry in Northern Ireland at that time? There have been subsequent generations of poets who have proceeded from your example – do you have particular memories of encountering those poets?

For me, it all began in Trinity College, Dublin, where I met my first great friend in poetry, Derek Mahon, and my future wife, Edna Broderick, who talked about poetry the way poets do. We lived poetry with great intensity. It was very exciting and exhausting. I got to know Eavan Boland and Brendan Kennelly as well, but with Mahon it was a head-on collision. When Edna got a job in the English Department at Queen's, I followed her home to Belfast. There I met my second great friend in poetry, Seamus Heaney; and he introduced me to James Simmons who had recently returned from Africa. Heaney engaged with Mahon and me just as we had jousted with each other. A convection current seemed to be carrying us upwards. We were listening to each other. We were trying to impress each other. We were getting better and better. In 1968 I met Paul Muldoon outside the wee museum in Armagh where Heaney and I (with David Hammond the folk-singer) were performing 'Room to Rhyme', a programme of poetry and song. Much later, Medbh McGuckian came to a reading I gave in Downpatrick. In the bar afterwards, over drinks, she recited one of her poems, a cascade of brilliance. Frank Ormsby and Ciaran Carson have long been part of my creative life. I think we were a bit like the French Impressionists, a coincidence of talents, you might say, with our interactions multiplying the possibilities.

For a significant period, you worked at the Arts Council of Northern Ireland, on Bedford Street. Among your achievements there was the setting up of writer-in-residence programs at Queen's University, Belfast, and at the University of Ulster at Coleraine. That writers might enjoy a presence at universities is something recent generations have taken for granted. Did you meet any opposition to these appointments?

No opposition at all. In those days the Arts Council trusted me and let me get on with the job. I joined the Council in 1970. Among other things, I'm proud of the writer-in-residence posts I set up at Queen's and the University of Ulster, and the programme of readings by visiting distinguished authors (Robert Lowell, Hugh MacDiarmid, Yevtushenko among them) which Edna and I organised for more than thirty years for the Queen's English Society. Over the decades I have watched these initiatives come slowly to fruition in the Seamus Heaney Centre for Poetry. The Centre has inspired young poets like yourselves to write and read critically, and to take the initiative in organising pamphlet publication and your own readings downtown at the Sunflower pub. The Centre represents everything I believe in, everything I was working towards as an arts administrator for all those years. In consultation with Seamus, the Centre was founded in order to give poetry a permanent place in the university at a time when poetry was becoming less central to English studies, owing to the advance of literary 'theory'. The Centre's soul is the transcendental achievement of a great poet. Today, university managerialism may be the deadliest threat to poetry – as to the humanities more broadly.

We spoke recently about a poem you admired, 'Those Winter Sundays' by Robert Hayden. Are you as likely now to encounter poems that surprise you, or poems that you admire, as you always have been?

I love that poem, especially its last line: 'love's austere and lonely offices'. A central excitement in my life is the discovery of brilliant poems that are new to me, for instance Gerald Stern's 'The War Against the Jews', Liz Berry's 'Bird'. It doesn't have to be a whole poem. At the very end of the fourth section of 'The Wound-Dresser', Walt Whitman remembers the young soldiers he had nursed as a medical orderly in the American Civil War:

> Many a soldier's loving arms about this neck have cross'd and rested,
> Many a soldier's kiss dwells on these bearded lips.

Just two lines, and I am airborne.

Notes on Contributors

Tess Adams grew up in Co Donegal and now lives in Surrey. She was joint runner-up in The Patrick Kavanagh Award, presented by the President of Ireland in 2014. She works as a psychotherapist, and is pursuing a Ph.D.

Mara Bergman's pamphlet, *The Tailor's Three Sons and Other New York Poems,* won the Mslexia Poetry Pamphlet Competition and was published by Seren Books, in 2015. *Crossing Into Tamil Nadu* won a Templar Quarterly Pamphlet Award, and was published in 2016. Her first full-length collection is forthcoming from Arc Publications, and she also writes for young children.

Eva Bourke, poet and translator, has published six collections of poetry, and several collections/anthologies in translation, most recently Moya Cannon's *A Private Country/Ein privates Land* (Edition offenes feld, 2017). She is co-editor of the anthologies *Landing Places: Immigrant Poets in Ireland* (The Dedalus Press, 2010), and *Fermata: Writings inspired by music* (Artisan House, 2016). Her seventh collection, *Seeing Yellow*, is forthcoming in 2018. She is a member of Aosdána.

Niamh Boyce won the 2012 Hennessy New Irish Writing Award for her poem 'Kitty'. Her novel *The Herbalist* (Penguin Ireland) was voted Newcomer of the Year at The Irish Book Awards in 2013, and long-listed for the International IMPAC Dublin Literary Award. Her poetry has been published in literary magazines and included in Raving Beauty's anthology, *Hallelujah for 50ft Women* (Bloodaxe Books, 2015).

Beverley Bie Brahic's collection *White Sheets* was a 2012 Forward Prize finalist; *Hunting the Boar* is a 2016 Poetry Book Society Recommendation. Her Apollinaire translation won the 2013 Scott Moncrieff Prize, and *Francis Ponge, Unfinished Ode to Mud* was a Popescu Prize finalist. A Canadian, she lives in Paris.

Matt Bryden runs the Somerset Young Poets competition, and is the author of *Night Porter*, which won the Templar Pamphlet Prize in 2010, and of *Boxing the Compass* (Templar Poetry, 2013), a first collection. The Poetry Map, a free online teaching resource, is accessible through his website at **www.mattbryden.co.uk**

Siobhán Campbell's books include *Cross-Talk* and her fourth collection *Heat Signature*, just published by Seren Press. She is widely published in journals, including in *Magma, The Hopkins Review, Poetry, Asymptote,* and *Poetry Ireland Review*. She holds awards in the National Poetry Competition and the Troubadour International Competition, and most recently was awarded the Oxford Brookes International Poetry Prize.

Gaius Valerius Catullus (c. 84 – c. 54 BC) was a Latin poet of the late Roman Republic, whose surviving works are widely read and translated.

Harry Clifton has published *Ireland and its Elsewheres*, lectures given during his tenure as Ireland Professor of Poetry, 2010-2013. *The Holding Centre: Selected Poems 1974-2004* and *Portobello Sonnets* were published in 2014 and 2017 respectively, both by Wake Forest University Press and Bloodaxe Books. He lives in Dublin.

Nan Cohen, the poetry director of the Napa Valley Writers' Conference, is the author of two collections: *Rope Bridge* (Lyre Poetry, 2005) and *Unfinished City* (Gunpowder Press, 2017). She lives in Los Angeles and teaches at Viewpoint School and the UCLA Extension Writers' Program.

Gerald Dawe has published eight poetry collections with The Gallery Press, including *Selected Poems* (2012) and *Mickey Finn's Air* (2014). *The Wrong Country: Selected Essays* will be published next year. He was a professor of English and Fellow of Trinity College until his retirement in 2017. He lives in Dún Laoghaire, Co Dublin.

John F Deane, born on Achill Island, has published many collections of poetry, notably *Semibreve* (Carcanet Press, 2015), and a memoir, *Give Dust a Tongue* (Columba Press, 2015). A new collection, *Dear Pilgrims*, is due from Carcanet Press in 2018. He founded Poetry Ireland and *Poetry Ireland Review*.

Craig Dobson has had poems published in *The London Magazine, The Rialto, North, Agenda, Stand, Orbis, Under the Radar, Butcher's Dog, Poetry Salzburg Review, The Interpreter's House, The Journal*, and poems in *The Boscombe Revolution* and *Bad Kid Catullus* pamphlets. He has work forthcoming in *New Welsh Review*.

Blair Ewing published two books of poems with Argonne House Press in Washington DC: *And To The Republic* and *Chainsaw Teddybear*. He has given more than 200 public performances of his work. His poems were recently published in *Abbey, Grasslimb, Bloodroot Literary Review, Gargoyle*, and *Poetry Salzburg Review*. His translations of Catullus have appeared in *Acumen, Lilliput Review, Poetry Salzburg Review*, and *The Federal Poet*.

Mary Gilliland hails from the northeast of the United States. Her poetry has appeared in such publications as *AGNI, Hotel Amerika, Notre Dame Review, Poetry, Stand, Tampa Review,* and has been anthologised in *Nuclear Impact: Broken Atoms In Our Hands* and *The &NOW Awards: The Best Innovative Writing.*

Colin Graham's poetry has recently appeared in *Banshee, The Tangerine, Lighthouse, The Pickled Body, Abridged, The Honest Ulsterman* and *The Literateur.* He is the author of *Northern Ireland: 30 Years of Photography* (Belfast Exposed, 2017); *Deconstructing Ireland: Identity, Theory, Culture* (Oxford University Press, 2001); *Ideologies of Epic* (Manchester University Press, 1998); and is co-editor of *The Irish Review.* He is curator of the Illuminations gallery at Maynooth University, where he is Professor and Head of English.

Erin Halliday's first collection *Pharmakon* was published in 2015 by Templar Poetry, and an ACES award from the Arts Council of Northern Ireland has enabled her to complete the manuscript for her second collection. She is the 2016 Ireland Chair of Poetry bursary awardee. Erin works as a course facilitator, teacher, and librarian.

Richard W Halperin's most recent collection for Salmon Poetry is *Quiet in a Quiet House* (2016). A new collection, *Catch Me While You Have the Light,* is forthcoming, also from Salmon Poetry. His most recent chapbooks for Lapwing Publications are *The House with the Stone Lions* and *Prisms.*

Patrick Holloway is a young Irish writer living and working in Brazil. This year he won second place in the Raymond Carver Fiction Contest, and was shortlisted both for the Dermot Healy Poetry Prize and the Over The Edge New Writer of the Year Award, for poetry.

Joseph Horgan was born in Birmingham, England, of Irish immigrant parents. He is the author of three collections and a prose work. He is a previous winner of The Patrick Kavanagh Award, has received an Arts Council Bursary, was shortlisted for a Hennessy Award and nominated for a Ted Hughes Award.

AB Jackson's first book, *Fire Stations,* won the Forward Prize for Best First Collection in 2003. His latest collection, *The Wilderness Party* (Bloodaxe Books, 2015) is a Poetry Book Society Recommendation. The voyage of St Brendan forms the creative core of his Ph.D. from Sheffield Hallam University.

Maria Johnston lives in Dublin and has taught poetry and literature at a number of universities, including UCD and Trinity College, Dublin. Her reviews and essays have appeared in a range of books and journals. Her essay on Medbh McGuckian has just been published in *The Cambridge Companion to Irish Poets*.

John D Kelly began writing creatively in 2011. He was Highly Commended in The Patrick Kavanagh Award (2016), and won joint 'Silver' in the International Dermot Healy Poetry Competition in both 2014 and 2015, amongst other successes. His work has also featured in a number of literary journals.

Matt Kirkham's second collection, *The Dumbo Octopus,* was published in 2016 by Templar Poetry. The poem in this issue of *Poetry Ireland Review* is from an extended sequence about the life of twentieth-century mathematician Kurt Gödel, a project for which Matt Kirkham received an Arts Council of Northern Ireland Artist's Career Enhancement award.

John Liddy is the founding editor, with Jim Burke, of *The Stony Thursday Book*. He has published ten collections of poetry in English, three with Spanish translations, as well as books for children. His most recent book is *The Secret Heart of Things* (Revival Press, 2014). He was Limerick City of Culture Poet-in-Residence for July 2014, and co-edited, with Dominic Taylor, *1916-2016: An Anthology of Reactions*. A collection, *Madrid & Other Poems*, is forthcoming in Spring 2018 from Revival Press.

Susan Lindsay's poetry is published in her two collections from Doire Press, *Whispering the Secrets* (2011) and *Fear Knot* (2013), and in journals and anthologies – including the 2016 Irish edition of *The Café Review* in Portland, USA. She read for Poetry Ireland's Introduction Series in 2011, and facilitates New Conversations mediated by poetry.

Catherine Phil MacCarthy's collections include *The Invisible Threshold* (The Dedalus Press, 2012), *Suntrap* (Blackstaff Press, 2007), and *the blue globe* (Blackstaff Press, 1998). Her novel, *One Room an Everywhere*, was published by Blackstaff Press in 2003. In 2014 she received The Lawrence O'Shaughnessy Award for Irish Poetry, and she won the Fish International Poetry Prize in 2010. She is a former editor of *Poetry Ireland Review*. A poetry collection, *Daughters of the House*, is forthcoming.

Jaki McCarrick is an award-winning writer of plays, poetry, and fiction. Her debut story collection, *The Scattering* (Seren Books, 2013), was shortlisted for the 2014 Edge Hill Prize, and she has enjoyed international success with her play, *Belfast Girls*. Her poems are published in numerous literary journals, and she regularly writes for the *Times Literary Supplement*.

Afric McGlinchey's debut, *The Lucky Star of Hidden Things* (Salmon Poetry, 2012), was translated into Italian by Lorenzo Mari and published by L'arcolaio (2016). She received an Arts Award to complete her second, Forward-nominated collection, *Ghost of the Fisher Cat* (Salmon Poetry, 2016). Her work has been translated into five languages.

Eamon McGuinness is from Dublin. His poetry has appeared in *Boyne Berries*, *Looking at the Stars*, *Abridged*, *Skylight 47*, and *The Honest Ulsterman*. In 2017, he was shortlisted for the Strokestown International Poetry Prize. He holds an M.A. in Creative Writing from UCD.

Maitreyabandhu's first pamphlet, *The Bond*, won the Poetry Book and Pamphlet Competition, and was shortlisted for the Michael Marks Award. His debut collection, *The Crumb Road* (Bloodaxe Books, 2013), is a Poetry Book Society Recommendation. *Yarn* (also with Bloodaxe Books) was published in 2015.

Martin Malone was born in Co Durham, but now lives in Scotland. He has published two poetry collections: *The Waiting Hillside* (Templar Poetry, 2011) and *Cur* (Shoestring Press, 2015). His Great War-related third collection, *The Unreturning*, is forthcoming. An Honorary Research Fellow in Creative Writing at Aberdeen University, he has recently completed a Ph.D. in poetry at Sheffield University. He edits *The Interpreter's House* poetry journal.

Orla Martin has published poetry in *The Cúirt Journal*, *Crannóg Magazine*, and *The Stony Thursday Book*, and has had work shortlisted for the Jonathan Swift Creative Writing Award, the Gregory O'Donoghue International Poetry Prize, and The Francis Ledwidge Poetry Award. She works as the administrator at the Irish Writers' Centre, in Dublin.

Sighle Meehan is the author of *Maum*, a full-length, bilingual play produced by An Taibhdhearc for the Galway International Festival, 2015. She was the winner of the Imbas short story competition. Her poems have been published in anthologies and journals including the *Fish Anthology*, *Poetry for God, 1916-2016: An Anthology of Reactions*, *The Stinging Fly*, *Crannóg*, and *Skylight 47*.

Noel Monahan has won numerous awards for his writing. His poetry was prescribed text for Leaving Certificate English, 2011 and 2012. *Where the Wind Sleeps: New and Selected Poems*, is his sixth collection, published in 2014 by Salmon Poetry. *Chalk Dust*, a seventh collection, will be published in 2018, also from Salmon Poetry.

Patrick Moran from Tipperary has published three collections of poetry: *The Stubble Fields* (The Dedalus Press, 2001), *Green* (Salmon Poetry, 2008) and *Bearings* (Salmon Poetry, 2015). His poems have appeared widely in Irish outlets and also in the UK. He is included in *Windharp* (Penguin Ireland, 2015), an anthology of poems written by Irish poets since 1916. His fourth poetry collection, *Lifelines*, is due from Salmon Poetry in 2018.

Darren Morris has published poems in *American Poetry Review, The Southern Review, The Missouri Review, New England Review, North American Review*, and in other outlets. New work is forthcoming in *The National Poetry Review*. He lives in Richmond, Virginia.

Louis Mulcahy is a potter who writes poetry. He has three collections, one in Irish, all published by An Sagart Publishing. A fourth collection is ready for publication. He founded An Fhéile Bheag Filíochta in 2007, and was its Artistic Director until 2014. He holds an Honorary Doctorate from the National University of Ireland.

Scríbhneoir agus file dhátheangach é **Stiofán Ó Briain**. De cheantar an Lú ó dhúchas, spreagadh an oiliúint a bhfuair sé i Scoil na Gaeilge UCD é chun dul i mbun na filíochta i dtosach. Is san ollscoil a d'aimsigh Stiofán cumas agus grá don Ghaeilge, agus d'fhág an t-athshealbhú teanga seo rian mór ar a scríbhneoireacht. Bíogtar an iomad rudaí chun pinn é, ach is minic a bheireann síorchlaochlú an tsaoil, i gcúrsaí pearsanta, cultúrtha, agus náisiúnta, greim ar a mheanma agus ar a fhilíocht.

Elizabeth O'Connell-Thompson is the Literary Coordinator of the Chicago Publishers' Resource Centre and works for the Poetry Foundation. She is the author of *Honorable Mention* (dancing girl press, 2017), and her writing features in *RHINO, Entropy, The Best New British and Irish Poets 2017* (Eyewear Publishing), and elsewhere – see **https://EOTwrites.com**

Proinsias Ó Drisceoil's books include *Ar Scaradh Gabhail : An Fhéiniúlacht in Cín Lae Amhlaoibh Uí Shúilleabháin* (Clóchomhar, 2000) and *Seán Ó Dálaigh: Éigse agus Iomarbhá* (Cork University Press, 2007). He is the author of many essays on cultural history and on Gaelic poetry, literature and language of Ireland and Scotland, and on traditional song.

Lani O'Hanlon is a dance therapist. Her work has been published in *POETRY, Poetry Ireland Review, Mslexia, Southword, The Stinging Fly, The Moth, Skylight Poets, The Irish Times, Hallelujah for 50ft Women* (Bloodaxe Books, 2015), shortlisted for the Hennessy New Irish Writing Award 2017, and broadcast on RTÉ's *Sunday Miscellany*.

Francis O'Hare was born in Newry in 1970. He has published three volumes of poetry with Lagan Press – *Falling into an O*, *Somewhere Else*, and *Alphaville*. He has also published a collection of poetry, *Home and Other Elsewheres*, with Evening Street Press, USA.

Michelle O'Sullivan's first collection, *The Blue End of Stars* (The Gallery Press, 2012), won the Shine / Strong Award for best first collection. *The Flower and the Frozen Sea* (The Gallery Press, 2015) was a Poetry Book Society Recommendation.

Keith Payne is the Ireland Chair of Poetry Bursary Award winner 2015-2016. His collection *Broken Hill* (Lapwing Publications, 2015), was followed by *Six Galician Poets* (Arc Publications, 2016). Forthcoming from Francis Boutle Publishers is *Diary of Crosses Green*, from the Galician of Martín Veiga. A poet and translator, he shares his time between Dublin and Vigo.

Stav Poleg's publication credits include *The New Yorker*, *Poetry London*, and *Poetry Daily*. Her graphic-novel installation *Dear Penelope: Variations on an August Morning*, with artist Laura Gressani, was acquired by the Scottish National Gallery of Modern Art. She is an editor for *Magma Poetry*.

Eleanor Rees is the author of *Andraste's Hair* (Salt Publishing, 2007), shortlisted both for the Forward Prize for Best First Collection and a Glen Dimplex New Writers Award; *Eliza and the Bear* (Salt Publishing, 2009); *Blood Child* (Liverpool University Press / Pavilion, 2015); and *Riverine* (Gatehouse Press, 2015). She is a Lecturer in Creative Writing at Liverpool Hope University.

John Sewell recently moved to the Shropshire Hills. He is a prizewinner in various competitions, including a finalist in the Arvon. His collection *Bursting The Clouds* was published by Cape Poetry in 1998.

Stephen Sexton – see page 84.

Maresa Sheehan won First Prize in the Goldsmith Literary Festival Poetry Competition, and was Highly Commended in the Bridport Prize and the Over The Edge New Writer of the Year Competition. She is a vet, living in Carlow, and is working towards her first collection.

Gerard Smyth's poetry collections include *A Song of Elsewhere* (The Dedalus Press, 2015), *The Fullness of Time: New and Selected Poems* (The Dedalus Press, 2010), and *The Yellow River*, a collaboration with artist Seán McSweeney (Solstice Arts Centre, 2017). He is a member of Aosdána, and Poetry Editor of *The Irish Times*.

Stephen Spratt is an academic who writes poetry. He lives with his family on the south coast of England, and spends as much time as he can in West Cork.

Alan Titley is Emeritus Professor of Modern Irish in UCC. He is the author of novels, stories, plays, and poetry. His *An Bhean Feasa* (Cló Iar-Chonnacht, 2014), on the life and times of the Irish servant Goody Glover, who was hanged in Boston in 1688, is the longest poem in contemporary Irish.

Eamonn Wall's recent credits include work in *Cyphers, Cold Mountain Review*, and *New Hibernia Review*. He co-edited a special issue of *POETICA* (Tokyo) on 'Coleridge and Contemplation', and his *Junction City: New and Selected Poems 1990-2015* appeared from Salmon Poetry in 2015. Originally from Co Wexford, he now lives in Missouri.

Cathi Weldon is from Dublin and currently lives in Kerry. Her poems have appeared in *Cyphers* and in *Five Words* (ó bhéal). She also writes poetry in Irish under the Irish-language version of her name.

Grace Wells's debut collection, *When God Has Been Called Away to Greater Things* (The Dedalus Press, 2010), won the Rupert and Eithne Strong Award and was shortlisted for the London Festival Fringe New Poetry Award. Her second collection *Fur* (The Dedalus Press, 2015) was celebrated in *Poetry Ireland Review* as 'a book that enlarges the possibilities of poetry'.

June Wentland, born in Hull, holds an M.A. in Creative Writing, and is the Library Community Development Officer for Bath and N.E. Somerset. As an adult she has mainly written prose, but since carrying out a Larkin 25 commission in 2010, she has returned to writing poetry.

Simon West lives in Melbourne. He is the author of three volumes of poetry, and an edition of the Italian poet, Guido Cavalcanti. His most recent book, *The Ladder* (Puncher and Wattmann, 2015), was shortlisted for the Prime Minister's Literary Awards in 2016.

Joseph Woods, former Director of Poetry Ireland, is both a Patrick Kavanagh Award winner and a Patrick and Katherine Kavanagh Fellowship recipient; his fourth collection of poems, *Monsoon Diaries,* will be published by The Dedalus Press in 2018.